"The critical challenge for educators today is to successfully prepare s[...] don't yet know, and for jobs that don't yet exist. Schools must transfor[...] lifelong learners equipped to make thoughtful decisions. **Thinking Thro[...]** *is a valuable resource for teachers committed to helping students learn [...]"*

—Sherrill W. Parris
Assistant State Superintendent of Education
Alabama State Department of Education, Montgomery

"*Quality Questioning has provided an invaluable framework for our staff by supporting our adopting effective questioning practices and monitoring student response patterns school wide. Our faculty has found value in sharing and discussing the Quality Questioning practices and creating an environment conducive to inquiry and reflection. It is our belief that* **Thinking Through Quality Questioning** *goes beyond improving teacher practice to provide tools teachers can use to support students in becoming active, responsible learners through a reciprocal process of questioning, discussion, and response.*"

—Debbie Brooks
Principal
Cary Woods Elementary School, Auburn AL

"**Thinking Through Quality Questioning** *is an excellent resource for teachers who want to promote student thinking, engagement, and accountability for their learning. The power of this book is that it not only outlines teacher behaviors but it specifically connects them to student outcomes and behaviors. It truly supports the idea that student engagement translates into increased student learning!*"

—Jamalya Jackson
Director, Professional Development and New Teacher Induction
Hillsborough County Public Schools, Tampa, FL

"**Thinking Through Quality Questioning** *not only provides the tools needed to frame effective questions, it also provides the structures necessary to elicit thoughtful student responses and dialogue. The book guides educators through the process of creating a classroom rich in productive interactions by providing both practical examples and supporting frameworks.*"

—Jamie Parris
Director of Secondary Math and Science
Hamilton County Schools, Chattanooga, TN

"*Teachers and educational leaders will expand their students' thinking by doing what the authors so eloquently model in* **Thinking Through Quality Questioning***: focus on questions prior to teaching, create an environment for questioning, provide feedback and assist the learner in the development of their own thoughtfulness. It is remarkable to note that a book can model behavior! In an era of 'quick fixes' which result in short-term gains, quality questioning can support purposeful and thoughtful teaching and learning.*"

—Jody M. Westbrook
Executive Director
Texas Staff Development Council, Keller, TX

"*Anyone in an educational leadership position knows the pressure to do more with less.* **Thinking Through Quality Questioning** *reminded me that providing teachers with quality teaching tools is the best and most inexpensive means of improving teaching and learning. The book is clear, concise, and well-researched. As a recently retired superintendent, I can easily see this book becoming the focus for a year-long book study and professional learning experience.*"

—Joy B. Williams
Superintendent
Pierce County Schools, GA

THINKING
Through
Quality
Questioning

Deepening Student Engagement

JACKIE ACREE WALSH
BETH DANKERT SATTES

CORWIN
A SAGE Company

CORWIN
A SAGE Company

FOR INFORMATION:

Corwin

A SAGE Company

2455 Teller Road

Thousand Oaks, California 91320

(800) 233-9936

Fax: (800) 417-2466

www.corwin.com

SAGE Ltd.

1 Oliver's Yard

55 City Road

London EC1Y 1SP

United Kingdom

SAGE India Pvt. Ltd.

B 1/I 1 Mohan Cooperative Industrial Area

Mathura Road, New Delhi 110 044

India

SAGE Asia-Pacific Pte. Ltd.

33 Pekin Street #02-01

Far East Square

Singapore 048763

Acquisitions Editor: Hudson Perigo
Associate Editor: Allison Scott
Editorial Assistant: Lisa Whitney
Production Editor: Veronica Stapleton
Copy Editor: Codi Bowman
Typesetter: C&M Digitals (P) Ltd.
Proofreader: Scott Oney
Indexer: Rick Hurd
Cover Designer: Michael Dubowe
Illustrator: Mack Williams
Permissions Editor: Adele Hutchinson

Copyright © 2011 by Jackie A. Walsh and Beth D. Sattes

Printed in the United States of America.

Library of Congress Cataloging-in-Publication Data

Walsh, Jackie A.

Thinking through quality questioning : deepening student engagement / Jackie Acree Walsh, Beth Dankert Sattes.

p. cm.
Includes bibliographical references and index.

ISBN 978-1-4129-8902-2 (pbk.)

1. Inquiry-based learning. 2. Active learning.
3. Thought and thinking—Study and teaching.
I. Sattes, Beth D. (Beth Dankert) II. Title.

LB1027.23.W35

2011 371.3—dc22

2011009494

This book is printed on acid-free paper.

12 13 14 15 10 9 8 7 6 5 4 3

Contents

This chapter opens with a vision for a classroom where student thinking drives learning. Two frameworks are introduced. The first, around
which the book is organized, is a framework for teacher behaviors that
enhance student learning and thinking. The second is for student
thinking: a set of questions to guide and optimize student learning.

Featured in this chapter are five considerations for teachers who commit to becoming intentional in the preparation of quality questions:
(1) To what content standard does the question relate? (2) What is the
instructional purpose? (3) What is the desired cognitive level for student thinking? (4) In what context will the question be posed? (5) Does
the wording communicate clearly? Teacher-friendly tools are offered to
support teachers in formulating quality questions.

Teachers can use quality questioning to nurture and extend student
thinking, thereby helping students understand that true learning results
from thinking. Key strategies include using Wait Times 1 and 2 to allow
time for thinking, sequencing questions to scaffold student thinking,
and developing students' self-regulatory and metacognitive skills.

This chapter considers the use of quality questioning as formative assessment and offers strategies to help (1) ensure that questions meet criteria for formative assessments, (2) identify gaps between current and expected knowledge and skills, (3) provide effective feedback to students, and (4) use feedback to inform instruction.

The focus of this chapter is on strategies that assist students in assuming ownership of their learning. Using response formats that engage all students in thinking and responding is a basic way to heighten student response-ability. Others include using cooperative learning strategies, encouraging student questions, and using skillful discussion.

The vision of student learning presented in Chapter 1 will not take root and thrive without the intentional establishment of a classroom culture that welcomes—and demands—thoughtfulness. This chapter considers how various norms, introduced throughout the book, form the basis for a classroom culture in which thinking is expected, valued, and celebrated.

Preface

Twenty-two years ago, we collaborated with a group of teachers and school leaders to create a program of over-time professional learning for teachers. The program was known by its acronym, QUILT (Questioning and Understanding to Improve Learning and Thinking). While naming it, contributors deliberated over whether the *T* in QUILT should refer to teaching or to thinking. Thinking won. Originally, however, Understanding was not included in the program's title, which was simply **Qu**estioning to Improve Learning and Thinking. When Jackie reported that name to her family, her son Will, a fifth grader at the time, objected that the *U* didn't get full shrift. Several days later, he proposed that the *U* should stand for understanding because, as he said, teachers question so that students will think and understand. Then they will have truly learned. Almost a quarter of a century later, we continue to profess Will's wisdom: We question to engage students in thinking so that understanding and true learning result.

Six years ago, Corwin published our first book on questioning, *Quality Questioning: Research-Based Strategies to Engage Every Learner*. We organized the book around the QUILT framework and incorporated learning from the work we had done with teachers across the country. We continue to believe in the value of the QUILT framework and the research that underpins it. However, the knowledge base for Quality Questioning emerged from research on teacher effectiveness. Hence, the Quality Questioning framework focuses almost exclusively on teacher behaviors. Over time, our work and research in the field have convinced us that student behaviors, including the willingness and ability of students to ask questions, are perhaps a more important part of the thinking and learning equation than teacher questioning behaviors themselves. We subsequently incorporated this conviction and associated tools into the content of professional learning we facilitate for teachers.

A NEW FRAMEWORK

With the opportunity to write a new book on classroom questioning came the responsibility to reflect on our work in the field and to challenge our thinking. The result is the Framework for Thinking Through Quality Questioning, which is the organizer for this book. This new framework includes teacher behaviors, but each teacher behavior is connected to specific student thinking outcomes and behaviors. In effect, we turned our old framework inside-out and began our consideration of each behavior by reference to the results for students. The primary knowledge bases for this endeavor are those of cognitive science and the learning sciences. The former was still in its infancy when we began our work in questioning;

FRAMEWORK FOR THINKING THROUGH QUALITY QUESTIONING

Frame Quality Questions

- Determine content focus
- Consider instructional function
- Stipulate expected cognitive level
- Match to social context
- Polish grammar and word choice

Strengthen Student Thinking

- Expect thoughtful responses
- Afford time for thinking
- Scaffold thinking and responding
- Make thinking visible

Use Formative Feedback

- Employ questions to assess student progress
- Identify gaps between current and expected knowledge and skills
- Provide feedback to students
- Use feedback to inform instruction

Promote Response-Ability

- Hold students accountable
- Develop student capacity to ask quality questions
- Provide opportunities for students to learn collaboratively
- Teach skills of collaborative discussion

Nurture a Culture for Thinking

- Develop collaborative, caring relationships
- Teach and reinforce norms for questioning and thinking
- Adopt a language of thinking
- Cultivate habits of mind
- Celebrate breakthroughs in thinking

the latter had not yet emerged. While the Framework for Thinking Through Quality Questioning continues to draw on the teacher effectiveness literature, it is much more focused on the learner. This framework and accompanying strategies and tools are appropriate for all K–16 classrooms and all content areas.

The new framework, like its predecessors, is flexible and malleable, and we hope it, too, will withstand the test of time. It consists of five component behaviors, each of which, in turn, consists of a set of contributing behaviors.

ORGANIZATION OF THIS BOOK

Chapter 1 of this book presents a vision for student thinking and relates this vision to the Framework for Thinking Through Quality Questioning. Each subsequent chapter is dedicated to one of the framework's five components and its associated behaviors. We encourage you to read and reflect on the focus questions provided at the beginning of each chapter—and to return to them at chapter's end for reflection.

Included within each chapter are opportunities for reader reflection. These prompts, designated as "Thinking Through QQ," can help you think through your quality questioning (QQ) practices.

This icon signals these questions for reflection. We encourage you to read and respond to the prompts to connect the text to your personal and professional life.

You will also encounter norm statements throughout the text. These are quickly identifiable by the compass icon.

These are guides to teacher and student behaviors in classrooms committed to the use of quality questioning. We spotlight these norms because we believe that implementing them in a classroom is a first step toward improving questioning and thinking practices for all members of that classroom community.

Each of the first five chapters concludes with a section titled Connections: Developing Learner Capacity. These sections invite readers to explore the relationships between the component featured in the chapter and three variables associated with student learning and achievement: (1) student metacognition, (2) student engagement, and (3) student self-efficacy. Development of these three student variables can transform students into independent, lifelong learners equipped to make thoughtful decisions as citizens of a global community. The bridge icon indicates the beginning of each Connections section.

We continue our 25-year quest as actively engaged learners focused on quality questioning as it impacts teaching and learning. We learn through our reading and study of an ever-expanding knowledge base that informs the practice. We learn as we attempt to incorporate quality questioning practices into our teaching. We learn, most of all, as we observe K–12 classrooms and interact with educators across the country regarding their successes and challenges in using quality questioning with their students. We are continuing to think through and further develop our understanding of quality questioning, and we hope this book will support your efforts to do the same.

Jackie Acree Walsh

Beth Dankert Sattes

Acknowledgments

We gratefully acknowledge each individual who inspired, encouraged, and supported us throughout the process of conceptualizing and writing this book. Included among these are family members, colleagues, and our Corwin editor.

Hudson Perigo, Senior Editor at Corwin, was among the first who urged us to write a sequel to *Quality Questioning*. Hudson was there for us throughout this project, and we are grateful for both her insights and her patience.

The strongest impetus for this new book came from educators across the country who read and responded positively to *Quality Questioning*. Many of these attended professional learning sessions that we conducted on this topic and subsequently shared with us the difference this made for them and their students. While we cannot mention each one of these by name, we single out those who most directly contributed. Jennifer Barnett, teacher leader, Winterboro High School, Talladega County, Alabama, is a strong advocate for quality questioning and contributed a piece to this book that focuses on the use of questioning in project-based learning. Susan Holley, Associate Executive Director of the Texas Association of School Administrators, and Jody Westbrook, Executive Director, Texas Staff Development Council, have been instrumental in introducing thousands of Texas educators to quality questioning. Likewise, Cathy Gassenheimer of the Alabama Best Practices Center has played a similar role in Alabama. Without the enthusiastic advocacy of these and hundreds of their counterparts, we would not have begun this project.

We are extremely grateful for the graceful approach that our friend Carla McClure took to polishing our words as well as for the help of Carolyn Luzader in preparing the manuscript. How fortunate for us that Mack Williams agreed to render the delightful illustrations that pepper our book! We appreciate Mack's creativity and willingness to take on this project.

Last, and most important, we are thankful for the members of our families who put up with us and excused our grumpiness during the final days of the process. We acknowledge the love, support, and patience of Catherine, Will, and Stephanie Walsh and Lyle Sattes.

About the Authors

Jackie Acree Walsh, PhD, and Beth Dankert Sattes are longtime students and advocates of quality questioning for students, teachers, and school leaders. Authors of *Quality Questioning: Research-Based Practice to Engage Every Learner* (2005), they have provided professional development in classroom questioning for thousands of teachers and school leaders in more than 30 states. They are codevelopers of Questioning and Understanding to Improve Learning and Thinking (QUILT), a nationally validated professional development program on effective questioning, and copresenters of the Video Journal in Education series *Questioning to Stimulate Learning and Thinking* (1999). Included in their other joint endeavors are the creation of professional development modules on improving school culture (for the Southern Regional Education Board) and leading learning communities (for the Alabama Leadership Academy).

Jackie Acree Walsh holds a bachelor's degree in political science from Duke University, a master's degree in teaching (MAT) from the University of North Carolina at Chapel Hill, and a PhD in educational administration and supervision from the University of Alabama. Beginning her career as a high school social studies teacher, she has worked in university administration, at a state department of education, and as a research and development specialist at a regional educational laboratory. In recent years, she has worked as an independent consultant, specializing in design and facilitation of learning experiences for adults with an emphasis on questioning, classroom coaching, and leadership. Jackie can be reached at walshja@aol.com.

Beth Dankert Sattes holds a bachelor's degree from Vanderbilt University and a master's degree in early childhood special education from Peabody College. A former special education teacher, she worked in research and development at Edvantia (formerly AEL, a regional educational laboratory) in professional development and in parent and community partnerships with schools. Currently, she heads Enthused Learning, an educational consulting company, based in Charleston, WV, working with teachers and administrators on questioning, coaching, mentoring, and literacy. Beth can be reached at beth@enthusedlearning.com.

1

Framework for Thinking Through Quality Questioning

In What Ways Can Quality Questioning Advance Both Student and Teacher Thinking?

FOCUS QUESTIONS

1. What is our vision for students—the end we have in mind?

2. What are the purposes of quality questioning in today's classrooms?

3. What are the five critical components of quality questioning?

4. What is the relationship between quality questioning and student thinking?

5. How does quality questioning enhance student engagement and student self-efficacy?

Learning is a consequence of thinking.

—David Perkins (1992, p. 31)

Imagine your classroom being alive with students who confront new academic challenges by accessing and assessing personal knowledge and experiences related to the content at hand. Imagine these students making connections between new information and what they already know and asking questions when they sense a conflict between a preconception and a new concept or idea. These students set appropriate academic targets as they translate learning objectives into personal goals. They are able to articulate both what they are learning and why, and they connect classroom learning objectives to real-life opportunities and challenges.

These learners demonstrate curiosity, self-reliance, and perseverance, and they interact with their teachers, with one another, and with web-based and other resources as they engage in problem solving and meaning making. They ask questions to establish relationships between academic content and real-world phenomena. They also identify patterns within and across content areas; develop and test their hypotheses to better understand the ideas they encounter; and think deeply as they select and evaluate evidence, draw conclusions, and offer alternative ways of looking at issues.

These students understand that meaningful learning is a process that occurs over time, and they routinely monitor their progress in a variety of ways. For example, they process teacher formative feedback, skillfully use pre-established criteria or rubrics to self-assess and self-monitor, and reflect informally on their progress toward understanding new concepts. They are adept at consolidating their learning. Quite often, they conclude a unit of study with unanswered questions, which they then pursue on their own. These students exemplify learning that is marked by rigor (of thought), relevance (of content), and relationships (between existing and new ideas and among members of the classroom community).

Now, imagine this vision for student learning becoming a reality, this year, in your classroom, with the students you currently teach.

ENGAGING STUDENTS THROUGH QUALITY QUESTIONING

It's not your father's (or mother's) classroom anymore! The demands of our global society require a different type of teaching and learning, and nowhere is the needed change more evident than in the expanded role of classroom questioning. In the not-too-distant past, traditional teachers asked questions primarily to find out what students knew—usually, to evaluate whether students had committed to memory what was expected. And as most of us know from firsthand experience, teachers routinely called on one student at a time, expecting other students to observe quietly and wait for their turns. Typically, if a student did not answer correctly, the teacher called on another student, then another, until a "star pupil" (or sometimes the teacher) produced the expected response.

While some remnants of this practice remain, today's teachers know that this one-dimensional model does not tap the power and potential of quality questioning. Quality questioning, as defined in this book, is not a simple tool for extracting memorized information. Rather, it is a dynamic process through which a teacher intentionally engages students in both cognitive and metacognitive operations. The intended outcomes of such engagement are to help students with the following:

- Focus their thinking on specified content knowledge
- Use cognitive processing strategies to develop deep understandings and long-term retention of content
- Ask academic questions to clarify or extend understandings
- Monitor progress toward learning targets through self-assessment and use of formative feedback
- Develop personal response-ability by using structural supports for thinking
- Contribute positively to the creation of a classroom learning community in which thinking is valued

These student behaviors, like those envisioned in the opening segment of this chapter, exemplify student learning that is characterized by rigor, relevance, and relationships. Is this the reality in most classrooms? No. Do most students develop these cognitive skills and habits of mind automatically? No. Would most teachers welcome these students into their classrooms? Yes! Can teachers coach most students in developing these kinds of cognitive skills and habits of mind? Yes! Will it be challenging? Probably. Will it be worth the effort? Definitely! At least, we think so. But ultimately, that is a question for you, the reader, to explore as you read this book and incorporate its principles into your practice.

Our purpose in this book is twofold—in fact, we intend the title as a double entendre. First, we make a case that quality questioning is *the* primary catalyst for student thinking and learning. In developing this rationale, we elaborate on the components of quality questioning that cognitive scientists and teacher effectiveness researchers connect to increases in student thinking and achievement. Perhaps more important to practitioners, we offer specific tools and strategies that teachers and students can use to achieve the student outcomes described earlier.

Second, we hope to stimulate readers to "think through" the purposes and potential of quality questioning *and* to reflect on personal practice. To this end, we provide information and prompts to assist in personal reflection and collaborative dialogue focused on quality questioning. Here's our first prompt:

Thinking Through QQ: Reread and reflect on the vision for students that opened this chapter. Is this a vision that you and your colleagues can embrace? How would your students and their parents react to this vision?

COMPONENTS OF QUALITY QUESTIONING

Figure 1.1 presents a framework for teacher behaviors that promote thinking through quality questioning. This framework contains five functions that teachers execute to nurture and support student thinking.

These five functions are not sequential steps; rather, they are interrelated components of the dynamic process of quality questioning. Their placement in the graphic in Figure 1.1 is, however, intentional, as is their order in this book, which is as follows.

Frame Quality Questions

Quality questioning is not possible without quality questions; hence, the formulation, creation, or framing of the questions themselves is our first consideration. If questions are not aligned with instructional purposes and worthy of student thinking, then we need not bother with the other functions. In Chapter 2, we characterize the types of questions that stimulate student thinking and learning. We advocate for teachers working in teams to formulate focus questions as part of the instructional planning process. The chapter contains guidelines and tools for question formulation.

Strengthen Student Thinking

Even as we frame questions, we need to be thinking about the type and level of student response the question is inviting. What are the qualities of an acceptable response related to both content and cognitive demand? Planning for this function begins during the framing of questions, but selected strategies are executed live during class interactions. The goal is to scaffold students' thinking about both the question posed and their responses to it. This approach to processing a question differs radically from students' traditional approach to answering, in which they attempt to guess the teacher's

Figure 1.1   Framework for Thinking Through Quality Questioning

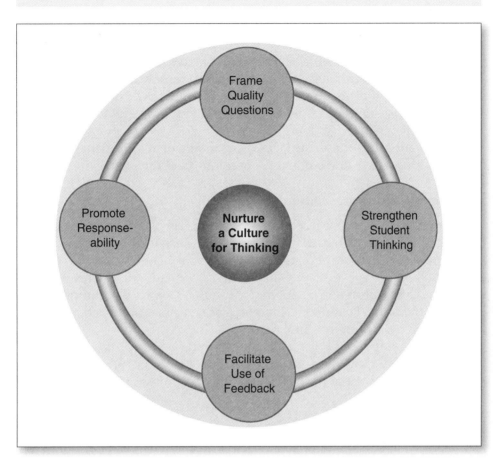

answers to classroom questions, which is what students learn to do in the "game of school." In Chapter 3, we review key strategies for supporting cognitive processing, including the use of Wait Times 1 and 2, the sequencing of questions to support students' thinking and answering, and the development of students' self-regulatory and metacognitive skills.

Use Formative Feedback

One of the most potent uses of quality questioning is for formative assessment that produces formative feedback for students—and for teachers. Many teachers are not skilled in identifying gaps in student learning revealed by their responses to classroom questions. Additionally, most students do not automatically know how best to use such feedback to manage their learning. Rather, both teachers and students usually think of teacher feedback as a simple evaluation of the correctness of their answers. In Chapter 4, we focus on questioning as formative assessment and provide strategies for using formative feedback to advance student learning and thinking.

Promote Response-ability

The goal is to engage every student in the classroom in thinking and responding through quality questioning and to build student ownership in this process. Attaining this goal requires a real shift in both teacher and student thinking—a shift from teacher control of student learning to a partnership approach that acknowledges each student's responsibility for managing his learning. Each of the previously discussed functions contributes to this type of response-ability. In Chapter 5, we examine strategies for developing student ownership for learning and thinking. Included among these are (1) use of various response formats, (2) encouragement of student questions, and (3) tools for assisting students in becoming self-directed learners.

Develop a Culture for Thinking

No matter how carefully teachers execute the technical aspects of quality questioning, student thinking will not thrive absent a culture to nurture and support it. Teachers and students partner to create a classroom culture in which thinking is expected, valued, and celebrated. The teacher and student behaviors featured in Chapters 2 through 5 provide the foundation for this type of culture. Featured in Chapter 6 are the norms and habits of mind that underpin a culture for thinking.

All five components of quality questioning are important; each promotes student thinking and, through it, student learning. Student learning, after all, is our principal focus, both in this book and in the classroom.

Thinking Through QQ: Review the Framework for Thinking Through Quality Questioning. How important to student learning do you believe each of the five components is? To what extent do you think about each of these components as you design lessons or units of study?

CONNECTIONS: DEVELOPING LEARNER CAPACITY

When students are given opportunities to engage actively in a curriculum that provides them with opportunities to be problem solvers, to make important decisions, to be creative, to broaden their knowledge base, to communicate their ideas, to consider alternatives, to be thoughtfully reflective, they flourish, not only in schools but beyond school as well.

—Craig Kridel & Robert V. Bullough Jr.
(quoted in Wassermann, 2009, p. 5)

Each component of the Framework for Thinking Through Quality Questioning embodies a set of behaviors, skills, and strategies that promotes mastery of content. Standards-based learning and achievement, after all, are the outcomes for which teachers and schools are accountable. Research-based practice can optimize the conditions for student learning. Ultimately, however, it is the student who learns or not. The sum of the performances of each individual student is society's measure of teacher and school effectiveness.

Not all students arrive in our classrooms equally prepared for academic learning. As we know, environmental factors give some an edge on their classmates. An often-referenced variable is existing background knowledge. We do not diminish its importance; however, the learner capacities explored in this book relate to thinking skills—both cognitive and metacognitive.

Specifically, we focus on these three powerful engines for student learning: (1) student metacognitive behaviors, (2) student engagement, and (3) student self-efficacy. The research and literature base for each one is massive, and it is increasing daily. Our purpose here is to encourage you to think about how you can use quality questioning behaviors to leverage all three.

Student Metacogntion

So what are the elements of student thinking that we expect to create as we attend to the components and principles of quality questioning? What behaviors or competencies are we seeking to develop in our students? And how do these thinking behaviors result in increased levels of learning and achievement? Our vision for student learning, presented earlier, is one response to these questions. It embodies six discrete elements of student thinking, each of which is presented below (and in Figure 1.2) as a question in the cycle of student thinking.

- **What am I seeking to learn or be able to do?** This question is the essential springboard for student entry into each new lesson or unit of study. If students are to manage and self-regulate their learning, they must know what they are attempting to master and why. And they need to be able to explain this in their own words—to formulate learning targets. This is key to students taking ownership

> In general, students are becoming more aware of their own thinking if they are able to describe what goes on in their heads when they are thinking. They can identify the kind of thinking they are doing, list any steps or procedures they are using to do it with skill, and can tell the pathways they took and the dead ends they met before they got to where they are in the sequence of steps.
>
> —Swartz, Costa, Beyer, Reagan, & Kallick (2008, p. 112)

Figure 1.2   Cycle of Student Learning and Thinking

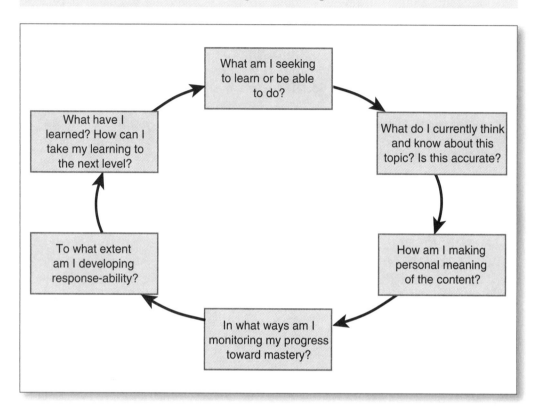

of their learning. Once they adopt learning targets, students are then able to establish interim goals for reaching these targets and to understand and use formative feedback from teachers.

- **What do I currently think and know about this topic? Is this accurate?** When students consider the first of these two questions, they activate prior knowledge, calling to mind experiences and understandings that they can then connect to new learning. When students consider the second question, they become more teachable; they open the door to the possibility that some of what they know may be inaccurate or incomplete. Effective teachers use diagnostic questions not only (1) to uncover misconceptions that need to be corrected before formal instruction begins and (2) to surface prior, accurate knowledge and understandings that students can tap into, but also (3) to assist students in learning how to manage self-assessment.

- **How am I making personal meaning of the content?** Thinking is the process of meaning making. To the extent that students connect to a topic under study in a personal way, they will find relevance and motivation for learning. Additionally, as they pursue learning about a new topic, they will engage in making connections with existing knowledge and experiences. Cognitive scientists are finding that these behaviors are at the core of moving information from short-term to long-term memory. As David Perkins (1992) writes, "Learning is a consequence of thinking" (p. 185).

- **In what ways am I monitoring my learning and progress toward mastery? Where am I along the path to reaching my learning targets?** This is the formative assessment question. Students answer it, in part, by receiving and processing teacher feedback; thinking students are also constantly self-assessing and self-monitoring. They have learned to self-regulate their learning.

- **To what extent am I developing response-ability?** Teachers who hold high expectations for student response-ability help students understand their role in using quality questioning to advance their learning and thinking. As students monitor their progress in this area, they are actually monitoring their development as lifelong, independent learners. This is a goal of many schools today: to create lifelong learners. Sometimes, however, neither teachers, students, nor parents know exactly what this means or what skills are involved. During this stage of student thinking, students are intentional in identifying and assessing behaviors that are associated with this outcome.

- **What have I learned? How can I take my learning to the next level?** This is the summative assessment for students. At the end of a unit of study (and at the end of a lesson), students need time and structures to bring some closure to a learning sequence, to consolidate their learning on the topic, and to set goals for future learning. Students, like teachers, need time for reflection if they are to improve their performance. Sometimes, these learning goals will foreshadow the next unit of study in the curriculum; at other times, they may point students to areas for individual and independent learning outside of school.

Most students do not come to school with these thinking skills, nor do they develop them automatically as they progress through school. However, research findings are clear that (1) students with these skills learn and achieve at higher levels than their peers, (2) students can learn these behaviors and skills, and (3) most students require direct instruction to develop these skills (Darling-Hammond et al., 2008; Holyoak & Morrison, 2005; National Research Council, 2001). Baker (2005) summarizes another important feature of metacognition: It is developmental, beginning in the early grades and maturing over time. Quality questioning can help develop and nurture the behaviors and skills of quality thinking.

The components and principles of quality questioning apply to instruction at all levels, pre-K through 16, and to all content areas. The cycle of student learning also applies to students of all ages in all learning settings.

> Metacognition develops gradually throughout childhood and into adulthood. It cannot simply be asserted that a child "has" or "does not have" metacognitive knowledge or control. Metacognition differs in degree and kind, and its relations with achievement change over time. The evidence is clear that children begin to use simple rehearsal strategies early in elementary school, but complex strategies for understanding text may not develop until middle or high school.
>
> —Baker (2005, p. 63)

However, the behaviors and skills comprising the student cycle develop over the course of a child's education.

Student Engagement

Quality questioning is a powerful vehicle for student engagement. This is particularly the case if we consider meaningful learning to be an acid test for authentic engagement. Phil Schlechty (2002) stipulates that authentic engagement results when the "task, activity, or work the student is assigned or encouraged to undertake is associated with a result or outcome that has clear meaning and relatively immediate value to the student" (p. 1). Linda Darling-Hammond (Darling-Hammond et al., 2008) reports that authentic engagement and learning include the following:

- Involving students in *"active learning, so that they apply and test what they know"*
- Making *"connections to students' prior knowledge and experiences"*
- "Diagnosing student understanding in order to *scaffold the learning process step by step"*
- *"Assessing student learning continuously"* and modifying teaching to meet student needs
- Connecting to "clear *standards,* constant *feedback,* and opportunities for work"
- "Encouraging *strategic and metacognitive thinking* so that students can learn to evaluate and guide their own learning" (p. 5)

Quality questions and questioning strategies support each of the previous in ways that we will elaborate on throughout this book. Unfortunately, not all educators can give a clear explanation of student engagement (City, Elmore, Fiarman, & Teitel, 2009, p. 11). This is true, in part, because we do not possess shared understandings of some of the critical concepts embedded in Darling-Hammond's (2008) listing.

To help readers reflect on the connections between questioning and engagement, we offer a schema that has been popularized by Richard Elmore (City et al., 2009, pp. 22–37) and colleagues at

> The search for meaning is at the very heart of motivation. Students must be inspired to wonder, develop intellectual curiosity, and desire to understand and find answers for themselves.
>
> —Hopkins (2010, p. 19)

the Harvard Graduate School of Education—the instructional core. Based on the work of Cohen and Ball (Cohen, Raudenbush, & Ball, 2003) at the University of Michigan, this schema (see Figure 1.3) consists of three fundamental elements of teaching and learning: (1) the student, (2) the teacher, and (3) the content. According to the theory, effective teaching and learning result from meaningful interactions between and among these three elements—and increases in student learning occur only as a result of improvement in these elements and in the relationships between and among them.

We argue that quality questioning activates and sustains interactions and relationships between students and teachers, between students and the content, and between teachers and the content in ways that increase both student engagement and achievement.

Figure 1.3 The Instructional Core

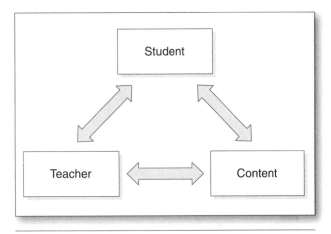

Source: City, Elmore, Fiarman, & Teitel (2009).

Thinking Through QQ: Speculate as to how quality questioning supports improvements in the instructional core. More specifically, how do you think quality questioning strengthens the relationships between and among the three components of the core?

Student Self-Efficacy

"I think I can; I think I can; I think I can." This refrain echoes from Mrs. Gaines' first-grade classroom, where Jackie began her school career, and from the pages of *The Little Engine That Could* (Piper, 1930), one of her favorite books from childhood. We all have stories that illustrate the power of believing in one's ability to accomplish a challenging task and in persevering to that end. Albert Bandura, a psychologist and researcher at Stanford University, focused on this phenomenon in his pioneering research. Bandura (2005) defines self-efficacy as "beliefs in one's capabilities to organize and execute the courses of action required to manage prospective situations," and says, "Efficacy beliefs influence how people think, feel, motivate themselves, and act" (p. 2).

Individuals with a strong sense of efficacy have a can-do attitude: They approach difficult tasks as challenges to be mastered rather than as threats to be avoided.

More specifically, individuals with a strong sense of self-efficacy are more likely to do the following:

- Approach threatening situations with confidence that they can exercise control over them. (These individuals are very different from those who lack this quality and seem to have acquired a sense of "learned helplessness" or a victim mentality.)
- Set challenging goals for themselves and maintain a strong commitment to them.
- Attribute failure to insufficient effort or a lack of knowledge or skills that can be acquired—rather than to a lack of ability, inferiority, bad luck, or other such factors.
- Increase and sustain their efforts in the face of failure.
- Quickly recover their sense of self-efficacy after a failure or setback.

Self-efficacy is positively associated with self-regulated learning, an important component of student metacognition. Researchers report that students who are self-efficacious establish higher goals for themselves and are more likely to select effective learning strategies than are their peers who are less self-efficacious (Schunk & Zimmerman, 1998, p. 3).

Bandura (2005, pp. 2–4) identifies four contributors to self-efficacy, all of which can be positively impacted by quality questioning:

- *Goal mastery.* When students set and attain challenging goals, they increase their feelings of efficacy. On the other hand, when students experience failure or do not have a clear view of learning goals or progress toward attainment, their feelings of efficacy suffer.
  - *Potential impact of quality questioning:* When teachers use questions to communicate clear expectations for student thinking and learning, students are better able to set short-term and long-term learning goals. Chapter 2, Frame Quality Questions, includes tools for the development of questions that promote this end.

- *Vicarious experience provided by social models.* Bandura writes that "seeing people similar to themselves succeed by perseverant effort raises observers' beliefs that they, too, possess the capabilities to master comparable activities" (p. 3).
  - *Potential impact of quality questioning:* In Chapter 5, Developing Response-Ability, we argue for intentional use of collaborative social contexts for student responding. When teachers plan for students' scaffolding of one another's thinking and responding, they are promoting and encouraging self-efficacy through social modeling.

- *Social persuasion.* Teachers and peers can influence a student's perception of self-efficacy by providing encouragement and meaningful feedback.
  - *Potential impact of quality questioning:* When teachers communicate to students that every student's answer is important and is a stepping-stone toward learning and mastery, students become more confident in thinking and answering. Chapter 3, Strengthen Thinking-to-Learn Behaviors, and Chapter 4, Use Formative Feedback, examine the ways in which a range of questioning behaviors encourage and reinforce students' belief in their abilities to learn standards-based content.

- *Physiological and social states.* According to Bandura's (2005) findings, one's feelings of comfort in a particular climate and with a given challenge can contribute to the development of self-efficacy.
  - *Potential impact of quality questioning:* Essential to classrooms where quality questioning promotes thinking and learning is a culture in which students (1) feel comfortable making mistakes, (2) exercise responsibility for supporting one another's learning, (3) demonstrate respect and trust for all in their learning community, and (4) cultivate habits of mind that support rigorous, relevant learning. Chapter 6, Create a Culture for Thinking, explicates these cultural qualities and connects them to student success.

Thinking Through QQ: Reflect on your experiences with students who may have been tentative or reticent about responding to questions. Identify one student whom you helped become a more forthcoming responder. What did you do to convey to this student that he or she possessed the capability to form responses to your questions?

2

Frame Quality Questions

What Are the Characteristics of Questions That Engage Students in Thinking and Deep Learning About Content?

FOCUS QUESTIONS

1. What are the qualities of student thinking and responding we expect to create through quality questions?

2. Why is it important to formulate questions as a part of the lesson planning process?

3. What are five key issues related to the framing of quality questions?

4. What tools and strategies can teachers use in crafting quality questions?

5. How does the context for answering influence the framing of questions?

> *More effort has to be spent in framing questions that are worth asking; that is, questions that are critical to the development of student understanding.*
>
> —Paul Black, Christine Harrison, Clare Lee,
> Bethan Marshall, & Dylan Wiliam (2003, p. 41)

Quality questions have one purpose: to engage students in interactions with their teachers and peers around the content under study so as to increase student understanding and mastery of curriculum goals. Such engagement requires that students be self-aware and active thinkers. Our challenge as teachers is to frame questions that result in this outcome.

Figure 2.1 conveys the end we have in mind for students whose teachers are asking quality questions. As teachers, we ask, *Are our questions resulting in these behaviors among the learners in our classrooms?*

The framing of quality questions that elicit such learning behaviors is a rigorous task that is best done collaboratively by teacher teams during the planning and design of instruction. Quality questions cannot be created on the fly during instruction, nor can the task of question formulation be separated from lesson planning. This is because quality questions are at the core of teaching, learning, and assessment. Their design cannot be left to chance. Teachers with whom we have worked over the years have confirmed our belief in the value of collaborative design. *"But wait!"* you might be saying . . .

"I don't have time in my schedule to plan questions before class!"

"What about the questions in the teachers' manual? I can easily lift and use those. They've served me well in the past."

"I don't like to be boxed in by predetermined questions. I prefer to go with the flow of my class."

If the idea of collaborating with colleagues to design questions is eliciting objections such as these, consider this: We define quality questions as a *limited* number of questions that teachers formulate as a part of lesson planning to trigger student thinking and to focus and engage students in the ways described in the opening paragraphs of Chapter 1. Teachers need prepare no more than two to five such questions for most daily lessons. By contrast, research indicates that teachers currently ask, on average, 50 questions an hour in elementary and secondary classrooms (Walsh & Sattes, 2005, p. 12). Therefore, what we are suggesting is a shift from quantity to quality. This shift will indeed require some extra time and effort, but as the saying goes, "Nothing worthwhile is quick or easy."

Figure 2.1 Expectations for Student Responses to Quality Questions

Content Mastery	Engagement	Cognitive Level	Interactions With Peers
• Demonstrates an understanding of the question itself, of what is being asked • Aligns answer with the content focus of the question • Includes correct factual, conceptual, or procedural knowledge in response • Finds relevance in content under study by relating it to content from other curricular areas and/or to life outside of school • Demonstrates an understanding of how metacognitive operations can support personal learning	• Listens actively to teacher or peer questions and comments • Asks questions to clarify, as needed • Demonstrates curiosity by asking questions, proposing experiments, suggesting possible resources for learning, and so forth	• Demonstrates an understanding of the level of thinking demanded by the question • Formulates an answer that is at the cognitive level intended by the question • Extends or elaborates on initial answer in response to teacher or peer prompts or probes • Builds on peers' answers to extend thinking to a higher level • Incorporates language of thinking into response; for example, uses verbs such as *speculate, theorize, compare,* and *contrast* in responses to questions • Is able to defend open-ended responses through rigorous analysis	• Supports other students' learning by providing explanations and offering direct assistance • Monitors participation in small groups; that is, speaks, but also encourages peers to speak • Demonstrates respect for other students and their answers, even when they are incorrect; when working in a collaborative group, seeks to scaffold peers' thinking to assist them in correcting an inaccurate understanding • Shows respect for divergent points of view when engaged in discussion around an open-ended question

Question formulation is a rigorous task because of its complexity and multidimensionality. Questions that lead to the behaviors depicted in Figure 2.1 result from consideration of five critical dimensions of question formation, framed here as questions for teacher reflection:

- On what content do we wish the question to focus our students? To which curriculum standard and related learning goals will the question relate?
- What is the function of the question in relation to student engagement and learning?
- At what level of thinking do we intend the question to engage students?
- In what social context will students be working (i.e., whole group, collaborative group, or individually)?
- How can we structure and word the question so that students will understand what is being asked?

Figure 2.2 provides a template for question design that includes each of these five dimensions. This template is a useful tool for individuals and teams of teachers engaged in framing quality questions.

Thinking Through QQ: Framing quality questions can be a time-consuming and rigorous task. Speculate as to the potential payoff to students and teachers from the use of quality questions.

DETERMINE CONTENT FOCUS

Initial thinking about a question begins with the *what*—the subject of the question. What concept, idea, principle, or phenomenon do we wish to have students think about? Decisions made about focus are the first determinants of the quality of a question as defined by rigor, relevance, and relationships.

One indicator of rigor is the alignment of a given question with the curriculum standards and learning goals that the unit or lesson addresses. Embedded in most standards are the four domains of knowledge identified in the **knowledge dimension** of the Revised Bloom Taxonomy

Figure 2.2 Template for Question Design

Focus	Function	Expected Cognitive Engagement	Context	Grammar
To which learning goal does the question relate?	**What instructional function is the question intended to further?**	**At what level of thinking will the question engage students?**	**In which social context will students be working?**	**What linguistic structure will best express the question?**
• What dimension of knowledge does the question address? **(Rigor)** ○ Facts ○ Concepts ○ Procedures ○ Metacognition • In what ways does the question connect to student readiness level, interests, and experience? **(Relevance)** • How does the question assist the student in making connections to prior knowledge—both	• *Essential Question* (integrating unit or lesson of study) • *Hook Question* (motivating/engaging) • *Diagnostic Question* (activating prior knowledge/conceptions) • *Check for Understanding* (conducting formative assessment) • *Probing/Scaffolding* (getting behind student thinking; assisting in concept development)	• Select a taxonomy to support your design of questions that are cognitively appropriate for the lesson and increasingly cognitively complex. • Teach your students about the different cognitive levels; then, hold them accountable for responding at each question's intended level. For example, the *Revised Bloom Taxonomy* (Anderson & Krathwohl, 2001)	• Individually? • With peers in a collaborative group or in parallel learning? • In a whole class or small group led by the teacher? In making a decision about content, the primary issue is the level of difficulty of the question and the potential for scaffolding of student thinking and learning. With independent work, the question needs to fall within a student's zone of proximal development; that is, questions should	Not all questions end with question marks! The choice of linguistic structure relates to the nature of the request for student performance. The following variations are appropriate for both oral and written questions: • A simple interrogative (e.g., *What were the primary contributors to the Gulf Oil Spill?*) • An eliciting statement or request for performance

(Continued)

19

Figure 2.2 (Continued)

Focus	Function	Expected Cognitive Engagement	Context	Grammar
within and across disciplines? **(Relationships)**	• *Inferencing* (drawing conclusions) • *Interpreting* (inviting analysis) • *Transfer* (using acquired knowledge or skills in novel settings) • *Prediction* (strengthening cause-and-effect thinking) • *Reflection* (supporting metacognitive thinking)	identifies the following cognitive operations: ○ Remember ○ Understand ○ Apply ○ Analyze ○ Evaluate ○ Create Other widely used taxonomies include Marzano's (Marzano & Kendall, 2006) *New Taxonomy of Educational Objectives*, Webb's (2002) *Depth of Knowledge*, and the tri-level Three-Story Intellect. (Walsh and Sattes, 2005)	be challenging, but not so difficult as to frustrate. Individual responding is most appropriate for practice and review. Peer-supported inquiry offers the opportunity for learning in a social environment with assistance from peers. Teacher-led questioning can serve as a tool for scaffolding more challenging and complex questions.	(e.g., *Speculate as to the primary causes of the Gulf Oil Spill.*) • A context-setting statement followed by a question (e.g., *On 4/20/10, an explosion occurred on the Deepwater Horizon platform. The media advanced various theories related to the cause. What do you believe to be two to four important causes leading to this explosion?*)

(Anderson & Krathwohl, 2001): (1) facts, (2) concepts, (3) procedures, and (4) metacognition. This knowledge dimension joins the **cognitive processing dimension** to form the Revised Bloom Taxonomy Table. The original Bloom Taxonomy was one-dimensional and, as we discuss later in this chapter, may have unintentionally blurred knowledge and thinking outcomes for teachers who used it. The Revised Bloom Taxonomy, presented in Figure 2.3, is a tool for clarifying both knowledge and thinking outcomes.

The authors (Anderson & Krathwohl, 2001, pp. 45–60) of this helpful frame for thinking about content focus characterize the four domains as follows:

- Factual knowledge includes knowledge of terminology, specific details, and elements.
- Conceptual knowledge encompasses knowledge of concepts, categories, classifications, principles, generalizations, theories, and so forth.
- Procedural knowledge subsumes knowledge of skills, algorithms, techniques, methods, and the like that are associated with a particular discipline.
- Metacognitive knowledge consists of knowledge about one's personal learning and thinking, self-assessment and self-monitoring strategies, and other strategic knowledge.

One's initial impulse might be to equate factual knowledge with lower levels of thinking. This is not necessarily so. Consider this question: *Hurricane Katrina and the Deepwater Horizon blowout both wreaked havoc on the American Gulf Coast. Compare and contrast the social and economic problems resulting from these two disasters.* Which domains of knowledge would a student call upon to answer this question? Certainly, students would need to know factual knowledge related to both incidents along with conceptual knowledge related to social and economic phenomena. The emphasis, however, would be on the facts of the two cases. Alternatively, teachers could ask students, *What were the results of Hurricane Katrina? In what ways did the Deepwater Horizon blowout affect the residents of America's Gulf Coast states?* These questions also focus on the factual knowledge associated with these two events.

Which of these questions is more likely to trigger student thinking? Which is more likely to assist students in processing the factual information and moving it to long-term memory? Which is more rigorous? If your response is the first approach, you are correct. The first question requires students to process the information at a higher cognitive level—in this case, to use the information to compare and contrast. Research findings are clear and consistent: When students use higher levels of cognitive processing to recode information and facts, they are

Figure 2.3 The Revised Bloom Taxonomy Table

The Knowledge Dimension	The Cognitive Process Dimension					
	1. Remember	2. Understand	3. Apply	4. Analyze	5. Evaluate	6. Create
A. Factual Knowledge						
B. Conceptual Knowledge						
C. Procedural Knowledge						
D. Metacognitive Knowledge						

Source: Anderson & Krathwohl, A TAXONOMY OF LEARNING, TEACHING, AND ASSESSING, Table 3.1 "The Taxonomy Table" p. 28, © 2001 by Addison Wesley Longman, Inc. Reproduced by permission of Pearson Education, Inc.

more likely to have long-term recall of the information (Hunkins, 1995, p. 20; Sprenger, 2005, pp. 66–79).

The knowledge domain does *not* determine whether or not a question engages students in high levels of thinking. Whether students think about facts, concepts, procedures, or metacognition (the four types of knowledge included in the knowledge domain), it is the expected level of cognitive engagement, which we consider next, that drives thinking. In our work with teachers over the years, we have observed that the original Bloom Taxonomy (Bloom, 1956) created some confusion by naming the lowest cognitive level "knowledge" and equating it with recall. Teachers rightfully protested that students need to be accountable for knowledge in order to perform well on high-stakes tests and to acquire a bank of knowledge required for successful functioning in our society. In fact, knowledge is the *what* of thinking at all levels; it does not represent a cognitive level. The Revised Bloom Taxonomy (Anderson & Krathwohl, 2001) eliminates this confusion by establishing two dimensions—knowledge and cognitive processing—and encouraging teachers to consider intersections between component parts of these two dimensions.

The first step in deciding upon content focus is to consult curriculum standards. The second is to consider ways you can make the question relevant to the students whom you expect to engage in thinking. Is there a connection between the curricular content and students' interests, experiences, and/or other subjects? Leila Christenbury, a secondary English educator, and her colleague Pat Kelly (1983), addressed this issue in their schema, Questioning Circle. This construct (see Figure 2.4) illustrates that teachers can help students connect most content knowledge to their lives outside of school and/or to content in another curricular area.

Let's go back to the questions about the Gulf Coast oil spill and Hurricane Katrina to consider possibilities for helping students think about the content under study (i.e., natural disasters) by connecting it to other facets of their lives. Here are a few possibilities:

The explosion on BP's Deepwater Horizon resulted in damage to the natural environment, including animal life. In what ways did the harm done to the Gulf's natural environment affect you and your family? Explain your answer. (Connection to personal life)

What are the properties of oil that cause it to harm wildlife? (Connection to other curricular area)

Many residents of New Orleans lost their homes and other property because of the flooding that resulted from the breaks in the levees. What is the purpose of a levee? Where are you most likely to find levees? (Connection to other curricular area)

Imagine that a force beyond your control damaged or destroyed something that you valued greatly. How do you think you would react to this loss? Why? (Connection to personal life)

Figure 2.4 Questioning Circle

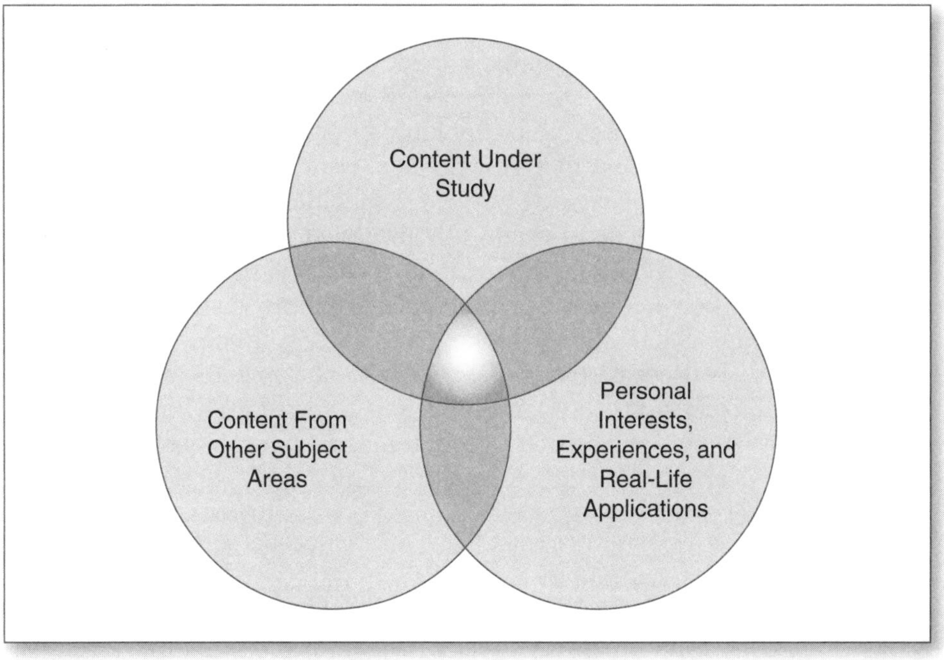

Content Under
Study

Content From
Other Subject
Areas

Personal
Interests,
Experiences, and
Real-Life
Applications

Source: Adapted from Christenbury & Kelly (1983).

For most teachers, the importance of making the various connections suggested by Christenbury and Kelly's (1983) Questioning Circle seems intuitive; indeed, the most recent findings of brain researchers and cognitive scientists confirm the value of such connections. These research findings demonstrate that long-term memory is enhanced when we make multiple synaptic connections between a given fact or concept and other information. Cognitive scientists refer to this as *knowledge integration* (Linn, 2009, p. 250).

CONSIDER INSTRUCTIONAL FUNCTION

Content focus is the springboard for question formulation. By attending to content focus, teachers determine the *what* of the question. The actual writing of a question begins as teachers consider the function they intend the question to perform. Teachers base their decision about the function of a quality question upon the instructional purpose it is to serve. Quality questions perform a myriad of purposes in any given lesson. Ten of the more common types of questions are described in Figure 2.5, and instructional purposes and sample questions are provided for each question type. The question types included in Figure 2.5 do not represent an exhaustive listing of instructional

(Text continued on page 29)

Figure 2.5 Types and Functions of Questions

Type of Question	Instructional Function	Examples
Essential Question • Is open-ended and conceptually based • Integrates facts around a main idea or concept	**Provides focus for a unit of study; can be used in lieu of an instructional goal or objective** • Engages students in thinking at the conceptual level and assists students in constructing schemata or mental models that assist in knowledge transfer • Assists students in finding patterns and making personal meaning • Promotes inductive learning by guiding students in discovery of ideas and their meaning • Helps students think at more complex levels (Erickson, 2002, pp. 90–91)	• *What are the limits of freedom?* • *Why do cultures differ in their definitions of beauty?* • *How can we uncover mathematical patterns?* • *How is our electronic culture affecting our brains?*
Hook Question • Is intentionally designed to spark student curiosity or interest • Has no single right answer • Lies at the heart of the lesson or unit • Is expressed in clear language that is understandable to students	**Motivates students to become actively engaged in new content** • Allows students to answer and become involved with content, even if they know little about it • Invites students to use their experiences, opinions, and creativity to connect to the content • Involves students in thinking and speculation • Encourages students to become investigators • Makes learning fun and adventuresome (Fried, 1995, pp. 78–80)	• *Assume you lived in the United States 200 years ago. Given your preferences and interests, what benefits or advantages would you have enjoyed compared with your life in today's society?* • *If you could be any creature of the sea, which would you choose? Why?*
Diagnostic Question • Addresses a critical component of unit and lesson design • Is often formed by teachers drawing on their experiences in teaching a concept to previous	**Activates prior knowledge and preconceptions related to a new unit or lesson** • Activates prior knowledge and beliefs (1) to enable determination of the correctness/incorrectness of these and (2) to allow students to connect new content to existing knowledge (assuming it is	• *In our geographic area, we experience four seasons. Locales that are closer to the equator do not have these seasonal changes. What is your understanding of why equatorial regions do not have our four seasons?*

(Continued)

25

Figure 2.5 (Continued)

Type of Question	Instructional Function	Examples
groups of students—forming questions around concepts and/or skills with which prior classes have had difficulty • Is most frequently posed and answered in writing or embedded in a Know, Want to Know, Learned (KWL) chart	correct) or (3) to engage in learning activities that will rectify misconceptions • Engages students in learning new content via connecting it to the known or to prior experiences • Provides teachers with information about student readiness to learn new content	• *This year we will be studying U.S. geography, including the locations of the 50 states and their capitals. List the names of all the states that you can remember. Place a checkmark beside any that you have visited.*
Question to Check for Student Understanding • Can be either planned prior to the lesson or asked spontaneously • If planned, teachers design it as a formative assessment to generate information that they can use to inform their next instructional move and that students can use to modify their learning strategies • When spontaneous, such questions may be asked when the teacher senses that students are not following the lesson logic and decides to verify this hypothesis	**Assesses the extent to which students are moving toward a learning target** • Allows teachers to assess student progress and to correct misunderstandings or fill in voids by providing additional instruction • Is one of the most accessible, easy-to-use, and productive types of formative assessment • Provides a mechanism for student self-assessment	• *What mathematical operations are used to determine earned run averages for baseball pitchers?* • *Why are there more cities with Spanish names in the western and southwestern parts of the United States than in other regions?* • *What rule of spelling is suggested by the following words: weight, neighbor, and reign?*

Type of Question	Instructional Function	Examples
Probing Question • Usually emerges during a teacher-to-student or student-to-student interaction • Focuses on the part of the student response that was incorrect, incomplete, or unclear	**Helps the teacher get behind student thinking and provide scaffolding for student learning and understanding** • Seeks to assist students in clarifying or extending an understanding (or correcting a misunderstanding) • Helps to scaffold student thinking, understanding, and learning	• *You stated that you do not believe in global warming. Help us understand how you reached this conclusion.* • *Previously, you told us that you think the early settlers mistreated the Native Americans. Provide specific examples of this mistreatment.*
Inference Question • Requires students to use evidence to draw a tentative conclusion • Focuses student thinking and is planned as part of lesson design • Asks students to synthesize information and suggest a probable outcome	**Asks students to go beyond the given information or evidence and draw a tentative conclusion** • Encourages students to find clues or evidence, analyze these, and make determinations about possible inferences • Asks students to fill in missing information • Promotes critical thinking	• *Television, in general, and 24-hour-news channels, in particular, has a dramatic impact on contemporary Americans' views of politicians.* • *Select one of the American presidents whom we have studied to date; read a biography of his life. Compose a two- to four-page essay in which you offer a scenario of how his political career might have been different had TV existed during his lifetime. Support your thinking.*
Interpretation Question • Asks students to make their own meaning of and/or personally evaluate content under study • Requires stipulation of criteria or standards on which the judgment or interpretation is based • May be more appropriate for a written response	**Solicits student analysis of a product (e.g., poem), an event (e.g., Potsdam Conference), or a big idea or concept (e.g., peace)** • Encourages independent thinking • Provides practice in evaluation or judgment • Permits students to form and express personal opinions based upon criteria	• *Review the lyrics of The Star-Spangled Banner. What do these words mean to you? What do you think they meant to Francis Scott Key, who composed this national anthem in 1814?* • *Which character in To Kill a Mockingbird do you think has had the greatest impact on readers over the years? Explain your answer.*

(Continued)

Figure 2.5 (Continued)

Type of Question	Instructional Function	Examples
Transfer Question • Requires students to apply information in a novel setting • Enhances relevance of learning if the new setting is connected to real-life situations to which students can relate	**Requires students to apply knowledge in novel settings** • Helps students internalize knowledge or move it to long-term memory • Provides students with a challenge, which can be motivating • Builds student confidence and self-efficacy	• This week we learned how to find the area of various geometric shapes. For homework, find the area of one room in your home. Use the yardstick we made in class to measure the dimensions of the room. Draw the room to scale on graph paper, marking dimensions. Then calculate the area.
Predictive Question • Engages students in if-then thinking • Is open-ended; there is no correct answer	**Facilitates student development of hypotheses** • Provides experience in forming evidence-based predictions • Assists students in cause-and-effect thinking • Vests students in the lesson	• Look at the number sequence listed below. Predict the next number in the sequence. • We have read the first half of the story. How do you think the story will end? Provide a rationale.
Reflective Question • Asks students to assess their personal relationship to the content they are studying • Should be planned to occur at strategic points in the lesson to encourage student ownership of their learning	**Causes students to think about their personal investment in learning and thinking** • Supports metacognitive thinking • Facilitates student self-regulation and self-assessment	• During this class, you often need to memorize certain facts. What strategies do you use to memorize material? What usually works best for you? • Think about your progress toward mastering the learning targets for this unit. What knowledge and skills have you learned up to this point? In what areas do you feel you need to spend additional time and effort to reach mastery?

purposes. Rather, as a body, they encompass the range of instructional purposes that teachers seem to emphasize.

Neither are the 10 question types and their accompanying instructional functions always mutually exclusive. For example, we have suggested the following question as a possible hook question: *Assume you lived in the United States 200 years ago. Given your own preferences and interests, what benefits or advantages would you have enjoyed compared with your life in today's society?* A hook question serves the function of activating students' curiosity and of motivating them to want to learn the content under study. We think that this sample question would pique the curiosity of a young person about to embark on the study of early 19th-century American culture. Some might argue, however, that this question is an example of an inference question because it requires students to find and analyze evidence and to use the evidence to draw tentative conclusions. Others might classify this as an interpretation question because it asks students to reach personal understandings regarding the daily life of someone their age during another time period—and to evaluate this in terms of their personal preferences. We agree that this question could serve any of these instructional purposes. It all depends upon the point in a lesson at which it is posed— and the teacher's expectations for student answers. Teachers ask hook questions near the beginning of a lesson or unit to motivate and interest students. They do not necessarily expect complete student responses to the question at this point. Teachers may return to the hook question throughout a unit—each time, having a different expectation for the student response.

Let us be clear that we do not offer this compendium of question types and functions to encourage classifying questions as to type. Rather, we created it as a tool for teachers to use in thinking and talking about the instructional purposes they seek to achieve through the crafting and posing of questions. We hope it will serve as grist for the mill as teachers seek to form questions to purpose.

> Good questions are clear in what they ask students to think about; they are not so broad or abstract that they defeat the process of thinking. Good questions invite; they do not command students to respond. Framing good questions requires the teacher to understand the purpose behind the questions; that is, does the teacher want to know what the students know or how students use what they know to understand?
>
> —Wassermann (2009, p. 26)

Thinking Through QQ: Skim through the question types and functions presented in Figure 2.5. Is there one (or more) that you do *not* use on a routine basis that is intriguing to you? Think about the potential benefits that your students might derive from regular inclusion of this question type in your classes.

STIPULATE EXPECTED COGNITIVE LEVEL

David Conley (2005) wrote *College Knowledge* to summarize the results of three years of research by 20 of the top institutions of higher education in the United States. The purpose of the investigation was to identify the skills and knowledge that students need to succeed in postsecondary education. Conley reports that a dominant theme in the resulting report was the importance of habits of mind such as critical thinking, analytical thinking, problem solving, and an inquiry orientation as well as the ability to evaluate source material, draw inferences and conclusions independently, and express oneself clearly both orally and in writing (p. 173). These closely mirror the thinking skills for the workplace found in the influential SCANS Report (Secretary's Commission on Achieving Necessary Skills, 1991). Today most experts agree that students require the same kinds of higher-level thinking skills whether they aspire to a college education or choose to go directly from high school to the workplace. They also concur that these skills should be developed over the course of a K–12 education; they cannot be taught in isolation or mastered just in time for high school graduation.

In the quest to move students to higher levels of thinking, most educators adopt a framework or taxonomy of thinking. Traditionally, the most commonly used framework has been the Bloom Taxonomy (Bloom, 1956). In 2001, Lorin Anderson and David Krathwohl edited a book featuring a revised version of the Bloom Taxonomy. Because most teachers with whom we have worked have a working knowledge of and experience with the original Bloom Taxonomy, we choose to highlight the Revised Bloom Taxonomy in our work and in this book. However, we know that a number of states use Norman Webb's (2002) Depth of Knowledge as the framework around which they organize levels of student thinking incorporated in their curriculum guides. Many teachers may also be familiar with Robert Marzano's (Marzano & Kendall, 2006) *New Taxonomy of Educational Objectives*. There are numerous other schemata for thinking about levels of thinking. Our view is that a district and its schools should adopt one such framework; it doesn't matter so much which one. What is important is that teachers and students have a common framework for thinking about thinking and that they use it in their collaborative work.

Why is it important to characterize student thinking by reference to a shared classification scheme? For purposes of quality questioning, we as teachers need to be clear about the type of cognitive processing a question requires prior to posing the question to students. If not, we are likely to accept any student answer that contains facts associated with the content focus of the question. Let's imagine that a teacher asks the following question: *The founding fathers decided to situate the U.S. capital in an area carved out of Virginia and Maryland. Evaluate the wisdom of this decision.* Let's further imagine this student response: *Washington, D.C., was situated in the southern*

United States because James Madison, Thomas Jefferson, and Alexander Hamilton reached a compromise.

The student response is correct factually, and a teacher might be tempted to accept this answer for that reason—especially if the responding student is usually nonresponsive or reticent to speak in class. Although the student's facts are correct, his answer did not include an evaluation of the short-term or long-term wisdom of the founding fathers' decision. Had the student's teacher determined in advance exactly what kind of thinking she wished the student to exhibit—and what that thinking would sound like—she would have been prepared to ask a probing question to assist the student in making a judgment as to the soundness of the decision. For example, she might have responded in the following manner: *You are correct that the location of Washington, D.C., resulted from a compromise reached by Madison, Jefferson, and Hamilton. Does historical evidence lead you to think that this was a wise decision? If yes, why? If not, why not?* This follow-up comment and question should push the student to think beyond the facts to the intended level—evaluation. Prior determination of the level of cognition suggested by the question would enhance this teacher's ability to scaffold student thinking to the expected cognitive level.

This scenario demonstrates one of the primary values of using a framework or taxonomy for thinking: to be intentional and specific about expected student cognitive processing. Regardless of the taxonomy being used, Figure 2.1 is a useful tool for carrying out such intentions. The column dedicated to "cognitive level" provides expectations for student responses that exhibit attention to cognitive processing.

The Revised Bloom Taxonomy

The Revised Bloom Taxonomy (Anderson & Krathwohl, 2001) offers a clear and understandable framework for thinking about both the knowledge and cognitive dimensions of questions. The knowledge dimension of the taxonomy was discussed earlier in this chapter. Our focus here is on the cognitive dimension.

As with the original Bloom Taxonomy, there are six levels of cognition identified in the revised taxonomy—from *remember* to *create*. In the revised version, verbs define each level of cognition, whereas in the original version the descriptors were nouns. We applaud this change because we believe that thinking is an action verb. The cognitive dimension of the Revised Taxonomy differs from Bloom's original in a number of other ways that we identify here.

Remember. Questions that call for recognition or recall of information are at the remember level. Recognition is the simplest form of remembering because it requires only that one locate information in long-term memory and match it with provided information. In this case, the presented information is a strong prompt for students. Recall, on the other hand, calls for retrieval of information without a direct prompt. Consider the difference between alternate response or matching items on a test and short-answer or fill-in-the-blank items. Note that the remember level applies to all four types of knowledge included in the Revised Bloom's knowledge dimension: factual, conceptual, procedural, and metacognitive. Remembering is not only about "just the facts, Ma'am." The following questions are illustrative of remembering:

- *What is the definition of algorithm?*
- *What is the algorithm for determining miles per gallon?*
- *Which amendment to the U.S. Constitution provided for women's suffrage?*

Understand. The authors of the Revised Bloom Taxonomy changed the root of the second level from "comprehend" to "understand," noting that understand is a response that teachers frequently give when asked about their objectives for student learning (Anderson & Krathwohl, 2001, p. 5). We believe the understand level of the revised taxonomy to be the richest and deepest of the six levels. Seven categories and cognitive processes comprise this level—more than twice the number of categories associated with any of the other levels.

Consider the power verbs defining the seven categories of understanding: *interpreting, exemplifying, classifying, summarizing, inferring, comparing,* and *explaining.* These verbs take a student far beyond the traditional definition of comprehension, which was "say it in your own words." In fact, these seven categories represent a range of cognitive operations. If a student truly understands—that is, can perform all seven of these operations—that student is grounded in the thinking skills that will enable her to move easily to the four higher levels. On the other hand, it can be counterproductive to ask a student who has not mastered understanding to engage in higher-level thought processes. In the zeal to push students to higher levels of thinking, teachers often feel pressure to ask questions at the highest levels before students have mastered basic understandings. Here are some examples of questions that solicit student understanding:

- *What does the Preamble to the Constitution of the United States mean to you?* (interpreting)
- *Which item does not belong: lettuce, corn, tomato, or broccoli?* (classifying)
- *What do you infer about the morality of the book's main character?* (inferring)
- *Compare the clothing worn by inhabitants of Alaska with that worn by individuals who live in Hawaii.* (comparing)
- *What contributed to the explosion on the Deepwater Horizon?* (explaining)

Apply. The third cognitive level is the bread-and-butter of many disciplines. It is also the level that, to many, ensures the relevance of knowledge. There are two categories of applying. One calls upon a student to apply a procedure to a familiar task in a comfortable setting (executing). The other asks students to implement a procedure in a novel situation or setting (implementing). The latter, the more rigorous of the two, is often referred to as transfer.

- *Determine the area of your desktop.* (executing)
- *What biases does the author of the assigned op-ed article reveal?* (implementing)

Analyze. Analysis is the true gateway to critical thinking. The conventional definition is to break something into its constituent parts to find out the relationship of the parts to one another and to the whole. Jackie's daughter Catherine recently provided a perfect example of analysis. Catherine, an art historian, was describing an assignment to one of her classes. The assignment was to execute a formal analysis of a selected painting. When Jackie asked just what this involved, Catherine stated that the students were to analyze the subject matter, style, and technique of the art object in order to make a judgment about how the work is represented. She noted that formal analysis requires the student to go beyond just describing an element to talking about its meaning and significance. This is, indeed, an exercise in critical thinking.

The Revised Bloom Taxonomy identifies three categories of analysis: (1) differentiating, (2) organizing, and (3) attributing. Differentiating engages a student in distinguishing between relevant and irrelevant or important and unimportant features of a subject. Organizing requires a student to decide how the various parts fit together within a structure. Attributing asks a student to determine a point of view. Catherine's assignment contained all three levels of analysis. Following are examples of questions that exemplify each level:

- *Consider the resources available to the American colonists as they waged the war for independence from Great Britain. Which resources do you think contributed most to the ultimate victory?* (differentiating)
- *What is the relationship of the various types of marine life in the Gulf of Mexico, one to another?* (organizing)
- *Reflect on your reading of* The Adventures of Tom Sawyer *and* The Adventures of Huckleberry Finn. *What common themes do you believe Mark Twain embedded in these two novels?* (attributing)

Evaluate. Evaluate was the highest level in Bloom's original taxonomy, but Anderson and Krathwohl (2001) demoted it one level in the revised version. They state that when students evaluate, they are manipulating existing knowledge, whereas creating (now the highest level) requires a student to go beyond given knowledge and fashion something completely new. Regardless, when students adhere to the highest standards of evaluation, they engage in truly rigorous thinking. Evaluative thinking demands not only that students make a judgment based upon credible evidence but also that they use criteria or standards to render the judgment.

The two categories of the evaluate level are checking and critiquing. Checking, which involves monitoring and testing, calls upon a student to find inconsistencies or fallacies within a product or process. Critiquing involves applying criteria for the purpose of making a determination of a product's relative value or worth.

Evaluation questions are relatively easy to craft but require rigorous assessment by the teacher to determine whether a student's answer meets the criteria for evaluation. Far too often, students provide opinions in response to evaluation questions—and these opinions are accepted. The caveat, then, regarding the asking of an evaluation question is this: Be certain that you determine in advance the criteria for an acceptable response because it is very difficult to make this judgment during the flow of a class. Here are examples of evaluation questions:

- *Using the rubric provided, assess the essay that you wrote in class yesterday.* (checking)
- *Rank-order the last four U.S. secretaries of state using the criteria for effective diplomacy that we created earlier during class. Be ready to explain your decision.* (critiquing)

Create. The final cognitive level involves students in putting together disparate parts to create a new product. Create supersedes what was called *synthesis* in the original taxonomy. Authors of the Revised Bloom Taxonomy have this to say about the create level and why it is above evaluate in the revised taxonomy:

The student must draw upon elements from many sources and put them together in a novel structure or pattern relative to his or her own prior knowledge. *Create* results in a product that can be observed and that is more than the student's beginning materials. (Anderson & Krathwohl, 2001, p. 65)

Create includes three categories or cognitive processes: (1) generating, (2) planning, and (3) producing. The following questions engage students in creating:

- *Generate a hypothesis to explain why students drop out of high school.* (generating)

- *Design a set of incentives to encourage individuals to conserve energy and participate in community recycling programs.* (planning)
- *Construct a website that will attract individuals who are committed to beautifying their local neighborhood.* (producing)

The six cognitive levels are further explicated in Figure 2.6.

Figure 2.6 The Cognitive Process Dimension

Categories and Cognitive Processes	Alternative Names	Definitions and Examples
1. Remember—Retrieve relevant knowledge from long-term memory		
1.1 Recognizing	Identifying	Locating knowledge in long-term memory that is consistent with presented material (e.g., Recognize the dates of important events in U.S. history)
1.2 Recalling	Retrieving	Retrieving relevant knowledge from long-term memory (e.g., Recall the dates of important events in U.S. history)
2. Understand—Construct meaning from instructional messages, including oral, written, and graphic communication		
2.1 Interpreting	Clarifying Paraphrasing Representing Translating	Changing from one form of representation (e.g., numerical) to another (e.g., verbal) (e.g., Paraphrase important speeches and documents)
2.2 Exemplifying	Illustrating Instantiating	Finding a specific example or illustration of a concept or principle (e.g., Give examples of various artistic painting styles)
2.3 Classifying	Categorizing Subsuming	Determining that something belongs to a category (e.g., concept or principle) (e.g., Classify observed or described cases of mental disorders)
2.4 Summarizing	Abstracting Generalizing	Abstracting a general theme or major point(s) (e.g., Write a short summary of the events portrayed on a videotape)
2.5 Inferring	Concluding Extrapolating Interpolating Predicting	Drawing a logical conclusion from presented information (e.g., In learning a foreign language, infer grammatical principles from examples)

(Continued)

Figure 2.6 (Continued)

Categories and Cognitive Processes	Alternative Names	Definitions and Examples
2.6 Comparing	Contrasting Mapping Matching	Detecting correspondences between two ideas, objects, and the like (e.g., Compare historical events to contemporary situations)
2.7 Explaining	Constructing	Constructing a cause-and-effect model of a system (e.g., Explain the causes of important 18th-century events in France)
3. Apply—Carry out or use a procedure in a given situation		
3.1 Executing	Carrying out	Applying a procedure to a familiar task (e.g., Divide one whole number by another whole number, both with multiple digits)
3.2 Implementing	Using	Applying a procedure to an unfamiliar task (e.g., Use Newton's Second Law in situations in which it is appropriate)
4. Analyze—Break material into its constituent parts and determine how the parts relate to one another and to an overall structure or purpose		
4.1 Differentiating	Discriminating Distinguishing Focusing Selecting	Distinguishing relevant from irrelevant parts or important from unimportant parts of presented material (e.g., Distinguish between relevant and irrelevant numbers in a mathematical word problem)
4.2 Organizing	Finding coherence Integrating Outlining Parsing Structuring	Determine how elements fit or function within a structure (e.g., Structure evidence in a historical description into evidence for and against a particular historical explanation)
4.3 Attributing	Deconstructing	Determine a point of view, bias, values, or intent underlying presented material (e.g., Determine the point of view of the author of an essay in terms of his or her political perspective)
5. Evaluate—Make judgments based on criteria and standards		
5.1 Checking	Coordinating Detecting Monitoring Testing	Detecting inconsistencies or fallacies within a process or product; determining whether a process or product has internal consistency; detecting the effectiveness of a procedure as it is being implemented (e.g., Determine if a scientist's conclusions follow from observed data)

Categories and Cognitive Processes	Alternative Names	Definitions and Examples
5.2 Critiquing	Judging	Detecting inconsistencies between a process or product; determining whether a process or product has internal consistency; detecting the effectiveness of a procedure as it is being implemented (e.g., Determine if a scientist's conclusions follow from observed data)
6. Create—Put elements together to form a coherent or functional whole; reorganize elements into a new pattern or structure		
6.1 Generating	Hypothesizing	Coming up with alternative hypotheses based on criteria (e.g., Generate hypotheses to account for an observed phenomenon)
6.2 Planning	Designing	Devising a procedure for accomplishing some task (e.g., Plan a research paper on a given historical topic)
6.3 Producing	Constructing	Inventing a product (e.g., Build habitats for a specific purpose)

Anderson & Krathwohl, A TAXONOMY OF LEARNING, TEACHING, AND ASSESSING, Table 5.1 "The Cognitive Process Dimension" pp. 66–67, © 2001 by Addison Wesley Longman, Inc. Reproduced by permission of Pearson Education, Inc.

Thinking Through QQ: The Revised Bloom Taxonomy (Anderson & Krathwohl, 2001) reorders the six cognitive levels introduced in the original taxonomy. What is your reaction to these changes? How might you be able to use the revised taxonomy as a tool for helping students better understand the different dimensions of cognitive processing?

MATCH TO SOCIAL CONTEXT

The traditional context for student questioning is the Initiation-Response-Evaluation-Follow-up model, in which a teacher asks a question of one student, evaluates the student's answer as to its correctness, and moves on to pose a question to another student. Wells (2001a) describes this as the "default option" to which most teachers almost always return (p. 185).

When teachers revert to the default option for asking questions, two student decisions strongly influence who will answer: (1) deciding whether to volunteer a response by raising (or waving!) their hands and (2) determining where to position themselves in the classroom, either in the teacher's action zone—across the front row and down the center of the room—or outside of this area. This pattern of classroom interaction allows a majority of students to assume the role of passive observers of classroom activity. It does not serve the purpose of engaging and developing *all* students' understanding. Unfortunately, the lowest-achieving students are the ones who typically choose to opt out of class interactions.

There are certainly occasions when teacher-led questioning in a whole-class setting is appropriate. Mike Schmoker (2011) makes a strong case for using interactive lectures and direct teaching, "where the focus is on the teacher's words and directions, but students take part in lots of pair-sharing, note-taking, or quick-writing" (p. 68). He emphasizes the importance of incorporating into these formats "guided practice, formative assessment, and ongoing adjustments to instruction" (p. 69). These practices require us to incorporate quality questions into such lesson formats. In Chapter 4, we offer suggestions for questions and questioning practices that support formative assessment and feedback.

Schmoker also advocates for whole-class discussion and debate when these are "tied directly to the posted learning goal or question and follow simple procedures that should be explicitly taught and reinforced like any good lesson" (p. 85). High-quality discussions and debates are products of carefully crafted quality questions and teacher modeling of supportive questioning practices. We focus on teacher and student skills and practices that promote effective discussion in Chapter 5.

When the whole class is the context for productive student interactions through questioning, teachers infuse lessons with strategies designed to ensure that *all* students are thinking about and formulating answers to all questions. Among such strategies are Think-Pair-Share and Turn-and-Talk, both of which ask students to form their own responses silently and then talk to a partner about their respective answers. Many teachers ask students to jot down a written response prior to calling upon a student to answer. Whatever strategy is used to afford students time to formulate their own responses, we advocate a "no hand-raising" policy. When this policy is instituted in the classroom, students know that the *teacher* will determine who is to answer, sometimes by using equity sticks (e.g., randomly selecting a student to answer by drawing a student's name—which may be written on a Popsicle stick—from a container).

Beyond the whole-class setting, teachers can choose from an array of other response formats that place students in different social contexts. Among the most common of these contexts are those in which students work

- individually, providing written responses;
- in pairs;
- in collaborative groups; and
- in a project-based learning environment.

Chapter 5 includes multiple strategies for use in each of these settings or contexts. All have value, and each is appropriate for some purposes and not for others. Teachers decide when and how to use these alternatives as a part of lesson planning.

Prior to framing questions, however, teachers should make decisions about which mix of contexts (and which specific strategies) they intend to use during a class period. All questions do not work equally well in all of these settings. For example, a teacher can pose a relatively long, complex question to students if it is presented in writing and students are asked to respond in writing. Such a question would not be appropriate for oral delivery in a whole-class setting. Likewise, questions crafted for use in collaborative groups will have distinguishing features determined, in part, by the size and composition of the group.

A number of guidelines can assist teachers in making the context decision. The primary issue for consideration is the level of difficulty of the question and the potential for scaffolding of student thinking and learning. Teacher-led questioning provides occasion for scaffolding or supporting student thinking and responding. Such scaffolding may be appropriate at any point in a lesson; however, it is particularly helpful during the early learning of new content or skills. At this juncture in learning, questions will appropriately check for understanding. When a student answers such a question incorrectly or incompletely, the teacher can immediately ask follow-up questions that reveal the missing piece of the student's knowledge or the faulty logic in his reasoning. This is an example of questioning for formative assessment and feedback, which is elaborated on in Chapter 4. These questions are most effective when tightly connected to key knowledge and skills, made succinct and understandable, and carefully framed prior to class to highlight important concepts.

With independent work, questions need to be challenging, but not so difficult as to frustrate. Individual responding is most appropriate for practice and review. Individual responding can also be used to activate the individual student's understanding or perceptions prior to work with a partner or in a collaborative group.

Both pairings and collaborative groups offer the opportunity for learning in a social environment with assistance from peers. More advanced students can support or scaffold the learning of classmates who may be less proficient with the knowledge or skills required for the learning activity. In this situation, the composition of the group is critically important. In fact, deciding upon group membership is one of the most challenging and important tasks teachers complete in the design of group work. Another factor related to effective group functioning is the choice of protocol or structure for the group work. Resource A includes a compendium of protocols that support productive group communications and interactions.

Once a protocol has been selected, the teacher can better frame questions. For example, a teacher might decide to use Think-Pair-Share to engage students in processing information presented in a lecture or teacher demonstration. For a 40-minute presentation, the teacher might formulate three questions. Because the purpose of the questions is to check for understanding, the questions should be closely connected to the content of the presentation, carefully worded so as to be clear and understandable when presented orally, and within the zone of proximal development of most members of the class (i.e., not too difficult and not too easy). On the other hand, a teacher might decide to employ the Jigsaw cooperative learning strategy to assist students in going deeper into one identified area of study. In this case, focus questions might be interpretive, predictive, or another type demanding higher levels of cognition. Likewise, because these questions are written, they can be lengthier and more complex.

Thinking Through QQ: For which of these social contexts do you plan most of your questions? Do you underutilize any of the five? Under what circumstances might you decide to experiment with this underutilized context?

A special category of collaborative group learning is project-based learning (PBL), an inquiry-driven approach that engages students in learning by completing activities that are relevant to the real world (Darling-Hammond et al., 2008; Krajcik & Blumenfeld, 2006). The success of PBL hinges on the quality of the questions that drive and structure student learning. Student projects begin with a driving question, a problem to be solved. As students pursue driving questions, they "use processes of problem solving that are central to expert performance" (Krajcik & Blumenfeld, p. 318) in the discipline they are studying, and they "learn and apply important ideas in the discipline" (p. 318) as they investigate their driving questions. Students work collaboratively, use a range of learning technologies to scaffold their work, and create products that demonstrate their learning. Krajcik and Blumenfeld (2006) report that students in PBL classes score higher on achievement tests than students in traditional classrooms.

Jennifer Barnett, a teacher leader at Winterboro High School in Alabama, writes in this chapter about the importance of framing quality questions in the PBL environment. Winterboro, a small, rural school, reinvented itself in one short year—changing from a traditional high school to a project-based school. At Winterboro, students engage in cross-disciplinary projects, and teachers team to facilitate student learning in technology-rich learning suites. The PBL learning environment permeates this school, where teachers work collaboratively to frame driving questions and essential questions (see Project-Based Learning: Framework for Understanding the Driving Question's Purpose, a feature article written by Barnett for this chapter).

PROJECT-BASED LEARNING: FRAMEWORK FOR UNDERSTANDING THE DRIVING QUESTION'S PURPOSE

A thesis is to an essay as a *driving question* is to a project. Just as a quality thesis statement provides a clear roadmap for readers, an effective driving question provides the foundation for a project. In a well-designed project, students create a final product or prepare a performance that answers the driving question.

Each task within a project must answer *essential questions* along the way that are related to the driving question. Essential questions help move students closer to being able to address the project's driving question. Carefully constructed tasks and activities encourage a gradual release of responsibility for learning to students, spurring independent investigation and inquiry. The entire project hinges on the quality of the driving and essential questions. Questions provide the focus students need to explore and create meaning of content and its relationship to the world.

HOW TO CRAFT QUALITY QUESTIONS FOR A STUDENT PROJECT

To craft quality questions, the first step is to unpack the standard to reveal what students must know. Then, teachers determine how that lesson relates to a student's world. This relationship (of the lesson to the student) begins the inquiry process. While concrete questions require analysis of empirical evidence, abstract and conceptual questions challenge a student's reasoning skills. Powerful questions for inquiry invite students to solve a complex problem or create a design effectively while meeting particular requirements. No matter the type, driving and essential questions must be provocative, open-ended, challenging, relevant, and linked to the core of what you want your students to learn.

EXAMPLES

Here are two examples of driving and essential questions that have been used with high school students. Each example includes a brief description of the related project designed to answer the driving question. Note that the driving question comes first and truly *drives* the project—not the other way around.

Example 1: Interdisciplinary (U.S. History/English)

Driving question

How far are you willing to go to achieve your dream?

Essential questions

History—How did the United States make the transition from an agrarian society to an industrial nation prior to World War I?

(Continued)

41

(Continued)

English—How does one recognize a fallacy in logic? How does one read informational and functional materials and evaluate strengths and weaknesses of arguments?

How the questions were answered

The class operated as families of four from various backgrounds (cowboy, Native American, homesteader, miner, immigrant, missionary, outlaw, etc.) and from a range of geographic locations.

As content was learned, "families" compiled digital scrapbooks and digital travel logs telling how they achieved their American dream.

Students wrote personal essays reflecting how the experiences of these pre–World War I Americans affect their own plans for achieving dreams.

Example 2: Math (Algebra I)

Driving question

How might data aid someone running for political office?

Essential questions

What are the various methods of reporting data? (for example, stem and leaf plots, histograms, line graphs, etc.)

What are the characteristics of a data set?

How does one determine the relationship of two sets of data using a scatterplot?

How the questions were answered

Groups of students created survey questions on community-related issues and administered the survey to 100 respondents.

Groups organized and interpreted data and related them to other sets of data.

The groups created a video advising a political candidate of their analysis and interpretation of the data collected.

Jennifer Barnett
Winterboro High School
Talladega County, Alabama

POLISH GRAMMAR AND WORD CHOICE

The fifth and final dimension associated with the framing of quality questions relates to the construction and wording of the question. If a student is to respond to a question, he must first understand what is being asked. Understandability and clarity relate to both the choice of vocabulary and the structuring of the interrogatory itself.

Whether presented to students orally or in writing, questions need to communicate. We have found that when we write out questions, we almost automatically edit for clarity and understandability. Even if our wording is somewhat awkward, the reader can usually decode the written word. However, when we deliver a question orally, clarity and understandability become more important because students must engage in auditory processing when the majority of students are visual learners. One solution is to project questions on a screen so that students can both see and hear them. We believe this is appropriate for lengthier, more complex questions that are intended to drive a discussion. However, we also believe that it is important for students to learn to listen in order to understand questions that are delivered orally. This brings us back to the need to ensure clarity and understandability.

Most of us do not craft clear, succinct, and understandable questions on the fly. We better conceive and clarify our thinking when we write. During our professional learning sessions on quality questioning, we ask small groups of participants to formulate questions, and then to elicit feedback from peers. We find the process of peer editing of questions to be a powerful one. When others read and talk about your questions, they are able to help you make them better. This is one of the reasons we strongly advocate that instructional teams craft questions during collaborative planning of lessons.

Thinking Through QQ: Reflect on the questions that you pose to your students. What percentage do you plan before class? Would your students say that your questions are clear, succinct, and understandable? What steps can you take to improve the linguistic quality of your questions?

 CONNECTIONS: DEVELOPING LEARNER CAPACITY

Our curiosity is provoked when we perceive a problem that we believe we can solve. What is the question that will engage students and make them want to know the answer?

—Daniel Willingham (2009, p. 20)

Questions build learner capacity when they assist students in moving toward a learning goal; intersect with their interests; and challenge, but do not frustrate, them. To the extent that we frame quality questions, we can enhance students' metacognitive skills, increase their engagement, and contribute to positive beliefs about their self-efficacy.

Student Metacognition

Students reap dividends at each stage in the cycle of student learning when teachers invest time and effort in the framing of quality questions.

- **What am I seeking to learn or be able to do?** Focused questions assist students in establishing a purpose for their efforts as they address this question.
- **What do I currently know or think about the topic? Is it accurate?** When teachers ask questions to assess students' prior knowledge and facilitate student self-assessments, they are concurrently helping students develop skills in self-monitoring, a critical skill for lifelong learners. As they encounter new learning opportunities, students automatically ask themselves these questions.
- **How will I make personal meaning of this content?** Teacher questions serve as models for student questions. A primary purpose of quality questions is to assist students in making personal meaning of a topic. As teachers, we need to remind students that meaning making is a powerful form of thinking—and that we pose questions to promote this end. Over time, students learn how to form these questions themselves and, thereby, formulate their own variations of and responses to the question.
- **How am I monitoring my learning and progress?** A large percentage of teacher questions in a quality-questioning classroom will be checks for student understanding of content and skills. These questions enable teachers to generate feedback that informs their instruction *and* student learning. The most effective checks for understanding engage students in self-assessing and monitoring their own learning and, thereby, give them practice in asking and answering.
- **To what extent am I developing response-ability?** As students begin to master metacognitive skills, they self-regulate both their learning and their strategies for learning. For example, they begin to assess the extent to which they are meeting expectations regarding their responding behaviors. They are able to provide evidence that supports their answer.
- **What have I learned? How can I take my learning to the next level?** Teacher questions assist students in self assessment, stimulate student curiosity, and may motivate students to answer a second query. As students understand and are able to practice self-monitoring and self-regulation strategies, they are more likely to ask themselves how they can take their learning to the next level.

Student Engagement

Questions, by nature, connect all components of the instructional core to one another. They engage students in thinking about the content that is their focus, and they connect students with their teachers as they respond to the cues embedded in the questions. If students understand what teachers expect them to do in response to a question, then they will be prompted to engage at a deeper and more meaningful level. Earlier (see Figure 2.1), we suggested that teachers communicate their expectations regarding student demonstration of content mastery, engagement, cognitive level, and interactions with peers. Teachers facilitate student engagement with questions when they are transparent about their expectations regarding student roles and responsibilities.

We can also enhance the quality of student engagement with questions by ensuring that we attend to the five dimensions of quality questions presented in this chapter. Consider the following:

- Questions that **focus** on the main ideas in the content under study (as opposed to questions that solicit random, disconnected facts) capture the interest of students—particularly when teachers help them connect this content to real life and to content from other subject areas through the use of the Questioning Circle, for example. When we craft questions that attend to this dimension, we bring rigor and relevance to student engagement.
- Identification of the **instructional function** or purpose contributes to a question's *raison d'être* and makes it more compelling to students. Remember the question types presented in Figure 2.2—essential question, hook question, interpretive question, predictive question, and so forth? Students can differentiate between these kinds of questions and questions that just "fill space" or that are "gotcha" inquiries. Quality questions have authentic purposes that provoke deep and meaningful student engagement.
- Quality questions challenge students to create personal ownership of academic content. They do this by engaging students at **appropriate cognitive levels** throughout a unit of study. Predicting, inferring, interpreting, and transferring information to a novel situation are more challenging cognitive operations than regurgitating, or simply recalling, information presented by the teacher or the text. We optimize student engagement when we are clear about expected cognitive outcomes.
- The **contextual dimension** is too often underutilized during the crafting of questions and planning of lessons. We know the power of peer-assisted learning and both the social and academic benefits of collaborative learning, but we too often revert to the teacher-centered, lecture-based classroom, which by definition excludes

students from active participation. Even when we use questions, we are typically hearing from only one student at a time. Situating questions in multiple social contexts produces variety and excitement, leading to higher levels of engagement for all students.

- Ultimately, the grammar of a question determines whether a student will understand and connect with it. A well-conceived, carefully worded, simply constructed question will quickly engage student thinking. On the other hand, most students will tune out a long, rambling question containing vocabulary that is too difficult or obtuse.

Student Self-Efficacy

When students engage in thinking about and forming their own answers to questions, their academic self-efficacy increases. It's just that simple—and that complex! Our argument is that meaningful engagement builds efficacy, or the belief that *what I do will make a difference in my achievement.* Our theory of action here is this: *If we as teachers spend time and effort crafting questions by reference to the five critical dimensions, then students will engage in thinking about and answering our questions, and then they will begin to believe that they can answer questions and master content, and then their performance and academic achievement will increase.*

The framing of quality questions contributes directly to goal mastery for students, one of the four factors associated with increasing self-efficacy. Quality questions do this in two distinct ways. First, a question that is well conceived, clearly focused, purposeful, and cognitively challenging communicates teacher expectations for learning outcomes, thereby facilitating student goal-setting. Essential questions exist for the purpose of communicating to students the focus and expectations for a unit. Daily focus questions that promote instructional purposes serve similar outcomes.

Second, carefully crafted and intentionally sequenced teacher questions assist students in monitoring their progress toward goal attainment. Students can use quality questions to chart their journey toward goal mastery.

Another factor that contributes to increased self-efficacy is increased student opportunity to address quality questions in collaborative settings. When students work in collaborative groups (whose compositions have been carefully determined by teachers), they have opportunities to vicariously experience positive peer modeling, another contributor to improved self-efficacy.

Thinking Through QQ: How can you help students understand that the ultimate purpose of quality questions is to support their thinking and learning?

3

Strengthen Thinking-to-Learn Behaviors

How Can Teachers and Students Use Quality Questioning to Deepen Thinking and Increase Learning?

1. Why is it important to convey to students the *what* and the *why* of thinking?

2. What is the value of teaching students how to use wait times?

3. How can teachers plan for scaffolding student thinking and learning?

4. What are some alternative approaches to making thinking and learning visible?

A major goal of most thinking interventions is to enhance learning and promote deeper understanding. The idea that deep and lasting learning is a product of thinking provides a powerful case for the teaching of thinking. Indeed, we venture that the true promise of the teaching of thinking will not be realized until learning to think and thinking to learn merge seamlessly.

—Ron Ritchhart & David N. Perkins (2005, p. 795)

Teachers today feel increased pressure to prepare their students with both (a) the knowledge and skills required for success on standards-based, high-stakes tests and (b) the skills and dispositions required for success in life and careers in the 21st century. Cognitive scientists present strong evidence to support the connection between learning content knowledge and learning how better to question and think. Why do many teachers believe these two challenges to be mutually exclusive? Why do teachers feel that they confront an either/or proposition—either prepare students for tests or teach them to question and think?

Our experience suggests that most teachers have not had access to the increasingly robust knowledge base emerging from the research of cognitive scientists. Few preservice or inservice teacher preparation programs do a good job of translating these findings to classroom practice. Further, merging thinking into the daily rhythm of classrooms requires a break with the past—and a break from the way we ourselves were taught. In *Education Nation*, Milton Chen (2010) shares this quote from Allen Glenn, dean emeritus of education at the University of Washington: "The biggest obstacle to school change is our memories" (p. 11). Chen continues: "We all think we know what a school is and how a classroom is organized, since we spent eighteen years in them during our formative years. It's hard to imagine anything else" (p. 11). If we are to take advantage of what Chen dubs "the thinking edge," we must, as he argues, change our views of the learning process and the roles of students, teachers, and parents in this process. We believe that more effective use of questioning can be the fulcrum for this change.

More specifically, we highlight four teacher behaviors that can nurture and support student thinking:

- Expect thoughtful responses.
- Afford time for thinking.
- Scaffold thinking and responding.
- Make thinking visible.

Each of these behaviors emerges from research and literature on effective questioning. Research from cognitive science expands and enriches each. The first two behaviors involve changes in deeply ingrained beliefs about roles, responsibilities, and rhythms in the classroom—on the part of both students and teachers. The most important desired outcomes for students are beneath the surface, largely invisible, because they occur in the students' minds. The third and fourth behaviors—scaffolding and making thinking visible—engage the teacher in constructing audible and/or visible supports for student thinking and learning. The resulting scaffolds and other concrete, overt structures direct and channel student thinking, particularly during the early stages of learning.

Thinking Through QQ: Educators, students, and parents all possess memories affecting their beliefs about how teaching and learning should occur. Identify one of these role groups (educators, students, or parents), and reflect on the extent to which your experiences with people in that group demonstrate the impact of their memories on beliefs. Then consider how we can respectfully address this barrier to change.

EXPECT THOUGHTFUL RESPONSES

Most students believe that teachers ask questions in class to surface the "right answers." When pushed, students will say that the right answer equates to the teacher's answer. Robert Fried (2005) includes the following in the first paragraph of *The Game of School*: "You had also better be ready to fake it properly when the teacher calls on you to answer a question to which you're sure he or she already knows the answer" (p. ix). In this book, he argues that few students are authentically engaged in learning in school; most learn how to play by the rules in order to get along and get by. Based upon our observations in hundreds of classrooms across the country, we must agree with Fried. Most students appear to be passive observers in class sessions during which teachers are asking academic questions. If called upon, these students try to provide the answers they think their teachers are seeking.

So how can we reverse this tide? How can we, as teachers, convince students that we intend our questions to be genuine vehicles for their learning? How can we communicate to them that we expect responses that reflect what they think and know about the subject in question so that we (and they) can use this information to move their learning forward? The short answer to these questions is this: We must teach our students these new behaviors; we cannot assume that they will figure them out by themselves. Only by being explicit regarding our expectations for answering will we begin to renorm our classrooms and schools and convince our students that we have a new way of doing the business of classroom questioning. So we recommend that you begin by talking with your students about the following norm.

Norm: Use teacher questions to **prompt** your thinking, not to guess the teacher's answer.

If students are to follow this norm, they must be clear about what thinking is and how it connects to retrieval of information needed to form a response to a teacher question. The following two simple definitions of thinking can be a beginning point for this conversation with students.

1. Thinking is the process of making personal meaning of information and experiences (Barell, 1995, p. 21; Hunkins, 1995, p. 7).

2. Thinking is the process of connection making—of relating a new fact, concept, or experience to what you already know and have stored in your long-term memory (Perkins, 1992, p. 8).

You might begin a dialogue with students by presenting these two definitions and asking them to reflect on each. Ask them to consider (1) what the two have in common, (2) whether they have ever been conscious of trying to make connections between new ideas and existing knowledge, and (3) if they have consciously attempted to make personal meaning when confronted with an academic task.

> Making meaning starts not with answers but with questions. Teachers who wish their students to be skilled at formulating their own meaning and their own understanding realize that lessons should frequently commence not with statements stressing answers but with questions posing puzzles.
>
> —Hunkins (1995, p. 7)

Information about how we learn and process information can motivate students to be more cognizant of their own thinking and how quality questioning supports it. Eric Jensen, Pat Wolfe, Renate and Geoffrey Caine, Judy Willis, and others are making research on brain-based learning accessible to educators. If you have pursued learning in this area, you can transfer this information to the task of helping students better understand thinking and questioning. While we have learned from each of these thought leaders, we focus here on the work of Daniel T. Willingham, author of *Why Don't Students Like School?* In this book, Willingham (2009) offers what he calls "just about the simplest model of the mind possible" (p. 11). It is the simplicity of this model that leads us to recommend it as a resource for increasing students' awareness of their thinking and learning. Figure 3.1 is an adaptation of Willingham's model.

In Willingham's (2009) view, working memory is "synonymous with consciousness; it holds the stuff you're thinking about," which is what you bring in from the external environment and what you retrieve from long-term memory. He writes that "thinking occurs when you combine

Figure 3.1 Model of How Thinking Works

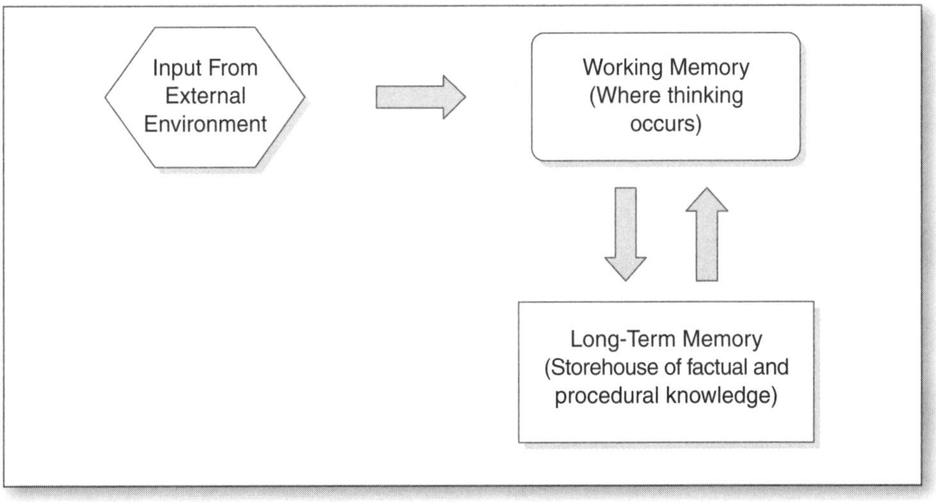

Source: Adapted from Willingham (2009, p. 11).

information (from the environment and long-term memory) in new ways" (p. 11). A teacher- or student-generated question comes to the working memory from the external environment. The question is a catalyst for activation of related facts and procedures residing in long-term memory, for bringing them into the working memory for processing. Teachers can use this model to help students understand how the mind works to make connections between a question and what they know about a topic.

Willingham (2009) emphasizes the importance of questions: "Sometimes I think that we, as teachers, are so eager to get to the answers that we do not devote sufficient time to developing the question" (p. 16). This was our point in the previous chapter: We as teachers need to attend to forming a challenging, interesting, and purposeful question if we are to engage our students' minds in thinking about what is being asked. We agree with Willingham that our questions need to embody puzzles, challenges, or problems that students are motivated to solve—and that they need to engage students at appropriate levels of difficulty. Should our questions fail to meet these two basic criteria, they will fail to trigger the kind of student thinking we are seeking.

As you present these ideas to your students, ask them about the characteristics or qualities of questions that cause them to think. Listen to your students. They will tell you the truth about these matters. We cannot expect them to think about our questions if our questions are not worthy of thought.

Thinking Through QQ: What are potential benefits of talking with students about their thinking and learning? Considering the characteristics of students with whom you work (e.g., their ages, grade levels, backgrounds, and so forth), how would you use this information to encourage them to think about questioning and thinking?

AFFORD TIME FOR THINKING

The first requirement for strengthening students' thinking-to-learn behaviors is to convince them that we are truly interested in their thinking by presenting them with questions worth thinking about and convincing them that we are interested in *their* answers. The second requirement is that we provide students with the time required for thinking—that we wait while they think about the question and formulate a response. Beginning with Mary Budd Rowe's discovery of wait time in the 1970s, researchers have amassed an impressive body of evidence-based support for the value of *think time*. To place Rowe (1986) and others' studies of wait times in the proper context, let's first consider what is required for a student to respond to a question aloud.

Answering, as we have already suggested, is a multistep process. It begins when students listen and attend to a question generated in the "external environment." If they are not attending to this stimulus, they will be unable to respond. The second step in the process occurs when they move the question into working memory and decode it to determine what is being asked. At this point, the brain also initiates the third step—a search in long-term memory to connect the question with knowledge previously deposited in that storehouse. When the brain makes a match between the question and relevant factual or procedural knowledge, this knowledge comes into the student's working memory. Now, the fourth step can occur, the thinking through of the question and relevant response data, and students can formulate an answer in their own minds. Only at this point are they ready to respond aloud in answer to the question. Figure 3.2 provides a model of this process.

Individuals process questions and generate responses at different rates and in different manners. Some are internal processors who prefer to have their responses formulated perfectly before saying them aloud. Others are external processors who are inclined to talk through their answers orally. The former require more quiet time for their processing; individuals who process externally are more likely to correct their answers as they are saying them aloud. No one approach is better or indicative of a higher intellect. Both require time for thinking—the first needs more time on the front end of the answering process; the second needs more at the end. Both groups benefit from the wait times first identified by Mary Budd Rowe.

Rowe (1986), a former science educator at the University of Florida, coined the term *wait time* during an investigation into the extent to which

Figure 3.2 The Process of Answering

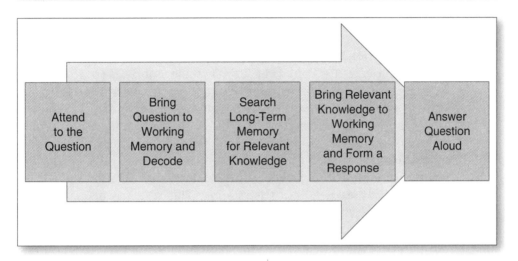

| Attend to the Question | Bring Question to Working Memory and Decode | Search Long-Term Memory for Relevant Knowledge | Bring Relevant Knowledge to Working Memory and Form a Response | Answer Question Aloud |

students in middle school classrooms engage in inquiry. Her particular interest was in finding out about their question asking and speculative thinking. To this end, she audiotaped more than 100 classrooms and coded student and teacher behaviors. What she heard was a lot of teacher talk; students seldom spoke, and when they did, they spoke in short answers. In fact, in only three classrooms did she hear student questions. She listened to the tapes once more to determine what the teachers in these classrooms were doing differently. She did, indeed, find one dramatic difference: Teachers whose students were speculating and asking questions occasionally stopped talking to allow time and space for student thinking and self-initiated talk.

As Rowe (1986) continued her research and began to focus on the silences in classrooms, she noted two particularly significant pauses. The first was the time that teachers waited after they posed a question before naming a student to respond. Rowe called this Wait Time 1. The second was the time that teachers paused after a student stopped talking when answering a question—before either giving feedback to that student or calling on another student to speak. She dubbed this pause Wait Time 2. She found that the threshold for both of these pauses was three seconds and postulated that the optimal time for both pauses is three to five seconds. She and other investigators identified a number of benefits that accrue to students whose teachers consistently use these pauses. A summary of the primary benefits follows.

Thinking Through QQ: What experience have you had with wait times—either as a teacher attempting to use them in your classroom or as a student whose teacher or instructor employed them? Was the use routine and consistent? What were the results?

Benefits Associated With Consistent Use of Wait Times

- **Students respond more correctly and completely more often.** Rowe's research revealed that, on average, 30% of students respond with "I don't know" to questions in classes where Wait Time 1 is not in use. This number drops significantly in classrooms where teachers and students use Wait Time 1 on a consistent basis (p. 45).
- **A larger percentage of students engage in answering questions.** Wait Time 1 also allows more students to enter the question-answering arena—most probably those students who are internal processors require more time to rehearse their answers before speaking aloud.
- **Responding students engage in higher levels of thinking, particularly in hypothesizing and speculating.** This was Rowe's particular interest as she championed inquiry-oriented classrooms. Both Wait Time 1 and Wait Time 2 support students' extended thinking.
- **Students are more likely to offer evidence for their answers.** Wait Time 2 appears to be particularly critical to this outcome. When students are given time to think and to retrieve more information from long-term memory, they can more effectively support their answers.
- **Students initiate more academic questions.** This was another of Rowe's special interests—the impetus for her initial research. Wait Time 2 affords the time and space in classes for student-initiated questions.
- **Classroom management problems decrease.** Teachers with whom we have worked are usually most surprised by this benefit, at least initially. However, when we ask them to speculate as to why the consistent use of wait times results in improved student behavior, they are quick with responses such as these: (a) *Many students act out when they are unengaged. Wait time gives them an opportunity for engagement.* (b) *If you wait for students to think and to answer, they sense that you care about them—and they're less likely to become discipline problems.* (c) *When students do not have time to think about a question and answer before a peer begins answering, they tune out and turn off or create disruptions.*
- **Students' confidence in their responses increases.** How often do your students respond to your questions with an inflection, or question mark, at the end of their answers? Most teachers agree that this is a common student behavior. However, when students experience consistent use of wait times over time, they become less dependent upon their teachers' evaluations of their answers and more confident in their own assessments.
- **Achievement increases on tests comprised of cognitively complex items.** A number of researchers, including Rowe, found that wait time nurtures students' oral responses to higher-level questions. When students have time to think, their answers are more likely to match the cognitive level of the question than are those of

their counterparts who do not experience the wait times. Tobin (1987) and others found that students in classrooms where wait times were employed also scored higher on written tests of cognitive complexity.

Source: Based on Rowe (1986).

Thinking Through QQ: Look back over the benefits outlined in this chapter. Which is most surprising to you? Why? Which would you most value for your students? Why? If you have been in a classroom where wait times were effectively used, did you observe these benefits? What is your evidence?

Helping Students Understand Wait Times

You can't simply "do" wait times "to" students—students are critical partners in implementing wait times effectively in their classrooms. This was perhaps our most significant learning during our early years of working with teachers to improve questioning practices. We believe there are multiple reasons for this, including the following:

- **The wait times, particularly Wait Time 2, will feel weird to students initially.** Students are accustomed to fast-paced classrooms in which there is typically only about one second of Wait Time 1 and virtually no Wait Time 2. When a teacher pauses—particularly after a student answers a question—most students are uncomfortable.
- **Students need to know what to do with the pauses.** Because this silence will be a new phenomenon to most students, many will require instruction in what to do with the silent time. You might simply ask your class the value, for example, of having time to think before someone is named to answer a question. Given the opportunity, students will speculate and develop sound hypotheses. Similarly, they can speculate as to the value of Wait Time 2.
- **Students themselves need to honor the wait times for one another.** This is exceedingly important in classrooms where students are working in collaborative groups or in project-based learning teams. In these contexts, students are responsible for monitoring their own behaviors, and they are in no less need of time to think as they engage in interactions with their peers.

There is no one best way to orient students to the wait times; your approach will depend upon a number of variables, including the age and grade level of your students and your personal teaching style. The important thing is to carve out time for conversations about wait times: what they are, why they are important for thinking and learning, and how students can use the time productively.

Thinking Through QQ: Have you ever talked with your students about the value of wait times? If so, what did you say to them, and how did they respond? If not, imagine how you would go about introducing or reinforcing the values of wait time with your students. Consider your students' ages, prior experiences, and other pertinent factors.

Following the orientation for students, we believe there is a need for scaffolding or supporting the use of wait times, particularly until they become somewhat automatic for both teacher and students. Here are some suggestions for promoting successful use of wait times by both teacher and students.

- **Provide opportunities for sheltered practice.** After you facilitate conversations about the what, why, and how of wait times, place students into groups of three to four and ask them to practice using wait times with one another. You may allow them to pose their own questions, or you might want to provide general-interest questions to them. Someone in the group should be the observer, whose task is to note the extent to which the speaking students honor wait times. The point here is to allow students to get the feel of the three to five seconds.
- **Use agreed-upon concrete signals to remind students (and yourself) of the wait times.** Some teachers raise one hand after asking a question and leave the hand raised for the three to five seconds. At the end of this time, they lower the hand and call upon someone to respond. We created a stop sign (see Figure 3.3) to use as a tangible signal of the wait times. One side of the stop sign is red and reads, "Stop and Think." The teacher holds this side up for three to five seconds following the delivery of a question before calling on someone. At the end of this time, she flips to the green side, which reads, "Listen and Learn." This is held up while a student is answering—and lowered three to five seconds after that student stops speaking.
- **Post norms and supporting wall charts to remind you and the students of procedures for using the wait time.** Posters such as those depicted in Figure 3.4 can be used to teach students about expected behaviors associated with Wait Times 1 and 2. These posters were adapted from two developed by Julie Porath, a second-grade teacher in Montgomery, Alabama, following one of our early trainings in quality questioning. They serve as visible reminders and can help scaffold student learning of skills related to wait time, which is difficult to use on a consistent basis, especially at first.

Figure 3.3 Signals for Regulating Wait Times

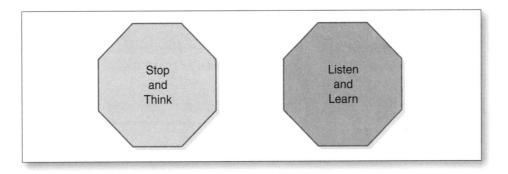

Figure 3.4 Expected Student Behaviors for Wait Times 1 and 2

Poster 1	Poster 2
Expected Behaviors for Wait Time 1	**Expected Behaviors for Wait Time 2**
What to Do When the Teacher Asks a Question	**What to Do During the Pause After the Responding Student Stops Speaking**
1. Listen carefully to the question. 2. Think about what the question is asking. 3. Use the silent time to match knowledge in long-term memory with the question. 4. Answer the question to yourself. 5. Instead of raising your hand, wait to be called on. 6. Be ready to answer in a public-speaking voice. 7. If you're not called on, listen carefully to your classmate's answer and think about it.	1. If you are answering the question, use the pause to think about what you said and add to or modify your answer. 2. If another student is answering, listen to understand what he or she is saying. 3. Use the time to compare your classmate's answer with your own. If there are differences, decide if you need to ask a question to clarify. 4. Be ready to ask your clarifying questions or "piggyback" by adding comments to what you've heard. 5. Demonstrate respect for your classmates, even when their answers are incorrect or different from your own.

- **During the early stages of use, ask students to reflect with you periodically as to how it's going.** To what extent is your community of learners consistently using Wait Times 1 and 2? How do they feel during the wait times? Are they, in fact, using these pauses to think? Do they have suggestions for improving classroom use?

Earlier we suggested a norm that can be used with students to remind them of teachers' expectations for thoughtful responses. We suggest the three norms that follow to communicate and reinforce behaviors associated with the two wait times.

 Norm: Use the pause following the asking of a question to think and to formulate your response.

 Norm: Use the pause after your answer to reflect and to add to it or change it.

 Norm: Use the pause following a classmate's answer to compare it with your own. Be ready to agree or disagree and to add your ideas.

Ideally, these norms are written on sentence strips—one per strip—and posted in conspicuous places around the classroom. They serve to remind both teacher and students of the commitment to a thoughtful classroom.

Students' commitment to thoughtful responses works in tandem with their use of Wait Times 1 and 2. If students believe their teachers' questions are for the purpose of finding out what they, the students, are thinking, they are more likely to value and use wait times. On the other hand, if they persist in the belief that teacher questioning is simply a fishing expedition designed to surface answers that are already in teachers' minds, they are less likely to persist in thinking about the questions. A sample wall chart (Figure 3.5) summarizes the expected student behaviors outlined to this point in this chapter. You can use this visual in introducing or reminding students of your shared commitment to behaviors that help everyone in the classroom community realize the potential of quality questioning.

Thinking Through QQ: How can you use the resources presented in this section to prepare and support students in changing behaviors?

SCAFFOLD STUDENT THINKING AND LEARNING

Correct, complete, and clear answers are not the norm in classrooms, even when teachers prepare and deliver quality questions and students are willing respondents. Oftentimes, when teachers pose questions—even those that are well formulated—students respond with answers that are not acceptable. This presents an opportunity for teachers, or classmates, to

Figure 3.5 Expected Changes in Student Behaviors

What Students Usually Do	What I Expect You to Do
Try to figure out "the teacher's answer" to a classroom question.	Think about what the question is asking and what you know or think about the topic. Be ready to respond with your answer.
Tune out if they are unsure of an answer.	Persist in thinking about what the question is asking, and identify what you know or think about the topic.
Raise their hands if they think they have the "right" answer.	Do not raise your hand, but be ready to respond with your answer if the teacher calls on you.
Become uncomfortable or embarrassed if the teacher or classmates are silent after they answer a question.	Use the pause after you respond to a question to think—and then add to your response or change it if you think it was incorrect.
Interrupt or try to speak immediately when they think they can add to or correct a classmate's answer.	Provide your classmates with time to think after they stop talking so they can extend or correct their responses.
Listen to the teacher's answers to questions, not to one another.	Listen to classmates' answers; compare your own answer to the speaker's; learn from one another.

assist the responder by providing follow-up questions or comments designed to scaffold the respondent's thinking.

The idea of scaffolding evolved from the work of Vygotsky (1978), who found that a teacher (or an experienced peer student) can help a student learn by identifying and delivering instruction that is within the student's zone of proximal development. This zone represents the appropriate target for student learning, the level of challenge or difficulty beyond current mastery that a student can handle. When teachers operate within the student's zone of proximal development, they present activities and assignments that are "just right" in terms of difficulty or challenge for the learner—neither too easy nor too difficult. Vygotsky's groundbreaking theory (see Figure 3.6) reinforces the importance of one characteristic of quality questions: They are of an appropriate level of difficulty.

Scaffolding is the help given to a learner that is tailored to that learner's needs in achieving his or her goals of the moment. The best scaffolding provides this help in a way that contributes to learning. For example, telling someone how to do something or doing it for them may help them accomplish their immediate goal; but it is not scaffolding because the child does not actively participate in the construction of knowledge. In contrast, effective scaffolding provides prompts and hints that help learners figure it out on their own.

—Sawyer (2009, p. 11)

Figure 3.6   Depiction of Vygotsky's Zone of Proximal Development

Knowledge and Skills
Already Mastered

**Zone of Proximal
Development**

Knowledge and Skills
Beyond Learner Readiness

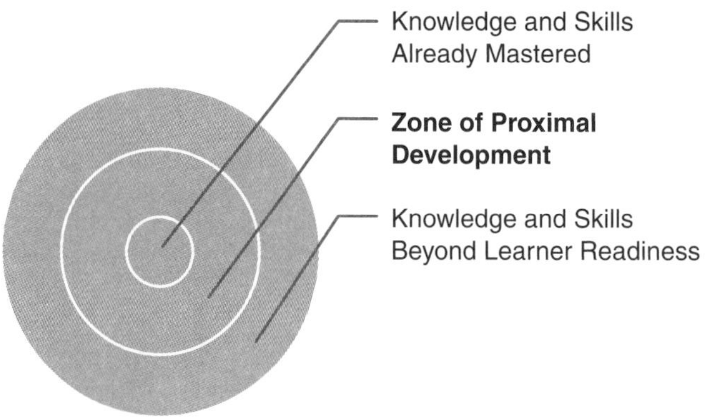

Source: Adapted from Vygotsky (1978).

Another concept related to scaffolding is the idea of a "gulf of expertise." Cognitive scientists frame the process of learning in terms of the learner's move from novice to expert and suggest that scaffolds support learner movement across the gulf (Quintana, Shin, Norris, & Soloway, 2009, p. 122). Building on the work of Piaget, they view learning as "an active, constructive process" during which the learners "create cognitive links from the new material to their own prior knowledge" (p. 122). These researchers are interested both in traditional scaffolding by teachers and accomplished peers and in software-based scaffolding. Our primary interest here is in traditional scaffolding, which involves structured questions and graphic organizers (Swartz, Costa, Beyer, Reagan, & Kallick, 2008, p. 80) as well as modeling (Quintana et al., p. 123). However, we know the power of software-based programs in individual scaffolding and encourage you to integrate these with questioning and coaching as you design a comprehensive approach to support your students.

While there are many definitions of scaffolding, we find the following particularly helpful as we think about the classroom culture or climate in which questioning as scaffolding best occurs:

Scaffolding involves (a) organizing participation in activities in ways that address basic human needs for a sense of safety as well as belonging; (b) making the structure of the domain visible and socializing participants for dispositions and habits of mind necessary for expert-like practice; (c) helping novices understand possible trajectories for competence as well as the relevance of the domain to the learners; and (d) providing timely and flexible feedback. (Blumenfeld, Kempler, & Krajcik, 2006, p. 491)

This definition emphasizes the centrality of student cognitive engagement to learning, but it also foreshadows two other components of our Framework for Thinking Through Quality Questioning (see Figure 1.1): facilitate use of feedback (Chapter 4) and nurture a culture of thinking (Chapter 6). Questioning to scaffold student thinking is productive only when conducted in a culture of openness, trust, respect, collaboration, and commitment to learning as a process. Chapter 6 has much more to say about this idea, but it is introduced now because of its critical importance. If students are to use teachers' follow-up questions to scaffold their thinking, they must perceive the questions and questioners as invitational, not interrogational. This requires the "sense of safety and belonging" in a learning community described by Blumenfeld and colleagues (2006). We suggest that teachers introduce the following norm to help acculturate students to this approach to questioning and thinking.

 Norm: Use follow-up questions to think about and self-assess your first response and to modify and/or extend your thinking.

In our work with teachers, we find the use of questions as scaffolding to be an extremely challenging proposition because it requires critical thinking in real time to create the prompts or probes that will assist the responder in clarifying, correcting, or extending his thinking. Teachers can use the three to five seconds provided by Wait Time 2 to formulate reactions to student answers. However, teachers report to us that when they think through possible responses to focusing questions prior to the class, they are better able to react to student answers in a productive manner.

Thinking through possible answers is a process that involves generating alternative responses and creating possible follow-up questions to less-than-optimal answers. We believe that this work is best done collaboratively, and we often provide this experience for teachers during our workshops on quality questioning. Figure 3.7 can be used as a template or worksheet for considering potential follow-ups to student responses.

Thinking Through QQ: Imagine that you are beginning a new school year and planning conversations with your students about your expectations for their engagement in classroom questioning. What would you like your students to know about scaffolding? How would you present this concept to them?

Figure 3.7 A Tool for Generating Expected Student Responses

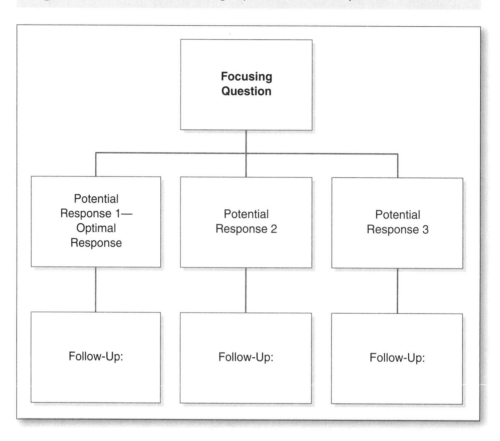

What kinds of follow-up questions assist students in thinking and learning? It depends on both the initial focusing question and the student answer. The following are some general guidelines that apply to all cases:

- **Hold the student accountable for responding with her best answer.** This aligns with the norm *expect thoughtful responses.* If a student answers *I don't know* or is simply silent, tell the student you want to hear her best thinking about the topic. Tell her that you need something to work with if you are to help her learn through the questioning and thinking processes.
- **Honor the student's answer by stating clearly whether it is right or wrong.** Avoid such comments as *Good try* or *This is a good beginning, but let's see if someone can help you out* or *That's not exactly what I was looking for.* These types of comments are given with the best of intentions, often to encourage a reticent speaker or low-achieving

student. The reality is that students know when a teacher is being less than honest with them or their classmates. Over time, as students receive such comments, they may come to believe that they are not truly capable of answering and that this is the teacher's way of dismissing them.

- **Distinguish between incorrect knowledge and incorrect cognitive processing.** Researchers report that, on average, teachers accept an estimated 50% of student responses that are at a lower cognitive level than the questions being asked (Ornstein, 1988). This may occur because teachers want to reinforce the correct knowledge embedded in the student response. It may also occur because, during fast-paced classroom interactions, the teacher is unable to assess the response and formulate a helpful prompt on the fly. This is the reason we recommend that teachers determine the parameters of an acceptable response as a part of the planning process prior to class. If they have this in mind as they listen to a student answer, they are better prepared to offer an effective reaction. Such a reaction reinforces the correct knowledge but scaffolds a student's reasoning or thinking to the appropriate cognitive level.

- **Following an incorrect or incomplete answer, begin follow-up moves by seeking to get behind the student's thinking, and try to understand why the student answered as he did.** If you are to assist a student in correcting a misconception or clarifying confusion, you need to know where the student's answer is coming from. Only when you understand the source of misinformation or faulty reasoning can you ask questions that will scaffold.

- **Use your best judgment in determining how long to stay with a student.** Teachers will need to determine how many prompts, probes, and assists to offer before providing the answer or moving to another student. When working one-on-one with a student in a coaching role, teachers can gently probe for an extended time—as long as the probing is fruitful. In a whole-class setting, it is important to provide assists. Scaffolding of the responder's thinking can help others in the class—especially when the classroom culture supports other students' listening and processing. However, there is a limit to how long a teacher can productively continue such assistance without losing other class members or embarrassing the spotlighted student.

- **If the student is unable to provide a correct answer, ensure that she hears a correct answer and explanation, and come back to her later in the class period.** The student may hear the correct answer from you or from a peer. The point here is to ensure that the student knows that the teacher will hold her accountable for this knowledge sooner, as well as later.

Thinking Through QQ: Reread the guidelines for follow-up questions designed to scaffold student thinking. Place a checkmark beside the ones to which you consistently adhere. Place a question mark beside any about which you have questions. Place an asterisk beside those that you'd like to incorporate into your practice.

In addition to these general guidelines for questioning to scaffold thinking, there are other ways to handle various student responses to questions posed at different cognitive levels. Here are some specific suggestions and examples.

Helping Students Make Connections to Answer Questions

Classroom questioning provides opportunities for students to review or practice recalling information from long-term memory. The accessing and processing of stored information in working memory promotes long-term recall. The more frequently we retrieve a memory, the more likely we can access it again (Sprenger, 2005, p. 139). You will remember from our review of the Revised Bloom Taxonomy (Anderson & Krathwohl, 2001) that recalling or retrieving is the more difficult form of the remember level.

We advocate asking more questions above the remember level because when we use information, particularly in novel situations, we are building different connections, thereby, strengthening the memory. However, there is a place in classrooms for simple remember questions, and there are strategies for teacher scaffolding of answers to this lowest cognitive level. Cueing and clueing are the most productive.

Cues trigger the brain to remember stored information. They can be communicated as words, symbols, places, or positions. They are simple devices introduced from the external environment (in this case, by the teacher) and designed to connect to a bit of knowledge in the student's long-term memory so as to bring it into the working memory for student response. Typically, a cue seeks to help the student connect something familiar (the cue) with the knowledge being learned—the knowledge elicited by the question. Consider the following example in which a teacher uses a cue to assist a student in learning a new vocabulary word.

Teacher question:	"What is the meaning of the word 'extraordinary'?"
Student response:	"I guess just common or everyday."
Teacher follow-up:	"You've defined *ordinary*, which is part of the word. This is *extra*ordinary. What does extra mean?"

| Student response: | "Oh, it means more or something added to. So I guess extraordinary must mean more than ordinary. Now I remember—it means different or unusual." |
| Teacher follow-up: | "That's correct. Do you see how you were able to use my questions to think through your answer?" |

The teacher questions elicit student knowledge from long-term memory and help the student combine two pieces of knowledge to create a new understanding. Cues can be even more overt. For example, the teacher might remind students of the place in a text where the knowledge appears, the day on which the class first studied a new phenomenon, or the steps that come before and after a step in a procedure. Cues that activate a visual memory can be particularly powerful.

Clues are even more obvious or blatant reminders. Think about this simple example:

Teacher question:	"What are human beings' five primary senses?"
Student response:	"Sight, hearing, touch, smell."
Teacher follow-up:	"Those four are correct. You have omitted one. Think about how you respond to ice cream."
Student response:	"Taste. Yes, that's it, taste."
Teacher follow-up:	"Correct."

This teacher might also have responded this way: *Yes, sight, hearing, touch, and smell are correct. In fact, when I think of the five senses, I think of being at the beach. I can see the awesome waves, hear them crashing, wade in and feel the water around me, and close my eyes and even smell it. I also know that the water is salty because of my fifth sense. Which sense would let me know about the salt?* Most students would be quick to respond: *Taste!* Think of the picture the teacher drew for his students and the new visual image he gave them for remembering the five senses. It is highly likely that this description will strengthen this knowledge for most of these students.

Questioning to Scaffold Thinking About Responses Beyond the Remember Level

Hopefully, you are asking an increasing number of higher-level questions in your class. As mentioned in Chapter 2, students are more likely to remember knowledge that they have had an opportunity to manipulate at the level of understand or higher. Also, as you may recall, we need to assess two dimensions embedded in higher-level student answers: the knowledge dimension and the cognitive processing dimension. Sometimes these two can bleed into one another: Faulty reasoning can lead to incorrect information, as in the next example. In this situation, a student is generalizing his personal experience to a particular case. This leads to a misconception, which the teacher addresses through a series of clarifying questions.

Teacher question:	"Albany, New York, like many other state capitals, is located on a river. Why are so many state capitals located on rivers?"
Student response:	"I think it's because people like to live around rivers because they are nice to look at and because they can do things like go fishing in them."
Teacher question:	"Can you tell me why you think this? I'd like to know why you think fishing and scenic views are connected with state capitals."
Student response:	"Well, my uncle lives in Nashville. I know that's the capital of Tennessee because he took me to the capitol building when I visited him. And my uncle's house is on the river. My aunt told me that they bought the house because she likes to look at the water and my uncle likes to fish."
Teacher question:	"This helps me understand what influenced your answer. But let's take a minute to think about the historic time when states decided on the location of their capitals. For example, the capitol building in Nashville was built in 1859. How many years ago was that?"
Student response:	"Um, let me think. That would have been more than 150 years ago. Right?"
Teacher question:	"Yes. Now, what do you know about how people traveled and transported food and other goods during the 1800s?"
Student response:	"I know that they didn't have automobiles, trucks, and airplanes. I guess they rode horses, traveled in boats, and sometimes by train."
Teacher follow-up:	"Now, tell me what happens in a state's capital city."
Student response:	"That's where laws are made and where the governor and other people come. Oh, I think I have an idea of why so many state capitals are located on rivers. They needed to be in a place where a lot of people lived and where other people could come and visit. People back then probably wanted to live on a river so they would be able to have boats to carry their goods and to travel. So states probably decided to

build their capitols in places where people already lived and where others could get to kind of easily."

Teacher follow-up: "You did think through your answer. You built on what you already knew and connected knowledge that you had to create a new understanding. Your inference is correct. State capitals were located on rivers for purposes of travel and transportation. The next time you visit with your aunt and uncle you can share your new learning with them—maybe while you're fishing!"

In this example, notice how the teacher gently challenges the student's assumptions and then provides prompts to help the student retrieve relevant prior knowledge in a sequenced fashion. This sequencing of questions assists the student in building a logic chain that will help the student when confronted with similar thinking challenges in the future.

Students do not always need intricate scaffolding to respond better to questions requiring higher-level cognition. Sometimes they only need more time to think and gentle encouragement. A number of prompts are great standbys for teachers when students are on a correct path but haven't moved their thinking to the appropriate cognitive level. In such situations, the following prompts can be particularly helpful:

- *Can you say more about this?*
- *I'm interested in your thinking about this topic. Can you continue to build on what you've said?*
- *You have already said _____, which is correct. Given the correctness of this line of reasoning, where would you go next?*

Sometimes students appear to have the knowledge to answer a question, but they are unable to articulate their thinking clearly. This happens when they overgeneralize and also when they get lost in their own thoughts and offer fuzzy or confusing statements. The following stems provide a beginning point for framing questions that assist students in clarifying and/or narrowing their thinking:

- *Can you tell me what you mean when you say _____?*
- *How are you defining or using the word _____?*
- *Can you express your main idea using different words?*
- *Can you give me an example?*

A widespread problem with student answers to open-ended questions is the tendency of students to offer their opinions without substantiating evidence or to parrot the opinion of someone else without thinking critically; for example, advocating an idea without using criteria to assess the soundness of the logic. We recommend that, prior to offering *evaluate* questions in a whole-class discussion or collaborative work environment, teachers review with their students the evaluate-level resources (such as the ones presented in Chapter 2). Help students understand what is involved in making judgments based upon criteria or standards. Give students practice in formulating criteria in a collaborative setting. Help them understand the difference between checking and critiquing, the two types of evaluation. Then, hold them accountable for their thinking by posing such questions as these:

- *What evidence do you have to support this judgment?*
- *What standards for assessment are you applying?*
- *Help me understand how this judgment is consistent with Criterion 1.*

Chapter 4 has more to say about how to use student responses to inform a follow-up teacher question to move thinking toward greater clarity, precision, and/or depth. Both scaffolding and feedback for thinking and learning improve when student thinking is visible. As discussed next, there are a variety of strategies for accomplishing this end.

Thinking Through QQ: What are your greatest challenges as you seek to get behind student thinking during a class discussion? What strategies have you found successful to achieve this end? Which of these techniques would you like to add to your repertoire?

MAKING THINKING VISIBLE

Visible Thinking is the name of a website hosted by Harvard University's Project Zero, which is codirected by David Perkins, a renowned cognitive scientist and thought leader. Dedicated to supporting integration of visible thinking into classroom cultures, the website (http://www.pz.harvard .edu/vt) offers a range of rich resources to assist teachers in this quest. Of particular value are thinking routines, protocols for student thinking that can be used in any content area or grade level. Perkins and his work have had a great impact on our thinking and our interactions with teachers around quality questioning over the years. Quality questions and quality questioning support visible thinking and learning. In combination with quality questioning, we use many of the thinking routines and graphic organizers offered by Project Zero and other like-minded think tanks to enhance student thinking.

> Teachers can help students change their original conceptions by helping students make their thinking visible so that misconceptions can be corrected and so that students can be encouraged to think beyond the specific problem or to think about variations on the problem.
>
> —Bransford, Brown, & Cocking (2000, p. 78)

In our view, three distinct sets of strategies can work in tandem with quality questioning to make thinking visible: (1) teacher modeling, (2) graphic organizers, and (3) thinking strategies and heuristics that support student metacognitive development. Provided here is a brief overview of these three, with specific examples for classroom use.

Teacher Modeling

The most accessible and visible form of classroom scaffolding is teacher modeling. Teachers can shift their presentational mode from one of telling to one of demonstrating how they think through a text, problem, or decision. Modeling is appropriate only when the individual doing the modeling is "proficient in applying a particular skill or habit of mind" and "demonstrate[s], step by step, how to carry out a thinking skill or demonstrates a habit of mind, explaining as it is applied how each step or behavior is done and why it is important" (Swartz et al., 2008, p. 79). Quality questioning is at the core of a number of well-defined protocols or strategies developed for this specific purpose, including think-alouds and reciprocal teaching.

Think-alouds. Elementary teachers have long known the value of think-alouds, particularly in literacy instruction. Through this strategy, teachers verbalize their thinking as they are reading a text aloud. The purpose is to make thinking visible to students so that they can learn from expert modeling. Israel and Massey (2005) have identified six distinct think-aloud strategies for use before, during, and after reading (p. 188). These strategies are illustrated in Figure 3.8 with sample questions appropriate for elementary school students whose teacher is reading *Charlotte's Web* (White, 1952).

As teachers pose questions during a think-aloud, they respond orally. After modeling think-alouds to their students, teachers begin asking students to think aloud during oral reading groups. In these settings, students can practice thinking aloud to develop their comprehension skills. Teachers provide feedback to assist learners in improving this type of cognitive processing.

Math educators often adapt the think-aloud strategy because, in mathematics, the focus is on the reasoning involved in solving a math problem. Typically, the teacher talks through the solution process in a step-by-step fashion, surfacing her thinking and encouraging students to think along with her. This scaffolding of student thinking allows students to participate in a more complex or difficult solution process than they would be able to execute independently (Silbey, 2002, p. 1). As in reading, teachers can engage students in the think-aloud process and gradually release control over the student's math talk.

Think-alouds are appropriate for students at all instructional levels and in most content areas. Two criteria for use are that the content be sufficiently authentic and complex and that it be thought provoking. One of the greatest limitations to implementation of think-alouds is teachers' lack of awareness of their own thinking and learning strategies. For example, to use a think-aloud in a literacy class, a teacher must surface, reflect on, and articulate his or her own reading strategies prior to modeling them for students.

Figure 3.8 Strategies for Think-Alouds

Think-Aloud Strategy	Sample Question
Before Reading	
• Activate prior knowledge	*This story is about Fern, a young girl who lived with her parents on a farm. Before I begin reading the story, I want to call to mind what I know about a farm.*
During Reading	
• Relate text to text	*It says on Page 8,* "Fern loved Wilbur more than anything. She loved to stroke him, to feed him, to put him to bed. Every morning as soon as she got up, she warmed his milk, tied his bib on, and held the bottle for him." *Earlier, we read that Fern had to teach Wilbur how to use the bottle. I'm remembering how Fern learned to take care of Wilbur. What exactly did Fern's mother do to help her with this?*
• Relate text to prior knowledge	*All babies require care from their parents. I'm calling to mind babies I know and what their parents do for them.*
	I'm asking myself how Fern's caregiving behaviors are similar to and different from those of parents I know.
• Infer	*While I was reading this chapter, I began thinking about why Fern's parents allowed her to have this piglet for a pet. What can I infer from what we know so far?*
After Reading	
• Use strategies such as summarize, predict, question	*Now that we've finished reading this chapter, I have a question: Will Fern continue to love Wilbur as much when he grows up?*
• Reflect	*I am really enjoying the story of Fern and Wilbur. I particularly like the way the author develops the characters. I feel as if I really understand Fern and Wilbur's relationship. I wish I could write a story that brings characters to life this way.*

Reciprocal teaching. Reciprocal teaching, another heuristic for making thinking visible, also comes from literacy instruction. Developed by Palincsar and Brown (1984), this process focuses on skill development in generating questions, clarifying, summarizing, and predicting. During the early stages of its use in a classroom, the teacher follows the protocol to engage students in an interactive dialogue around a selected text. As students become more adept at the process, the teacher gradually releases control and designates students to assume different roles in the process. The teacher monitors to provide feedback as students pursue the interactive dialogue.

As with think-alouds, the teacher selects a passage in the text for focus during reciprocal teaching; the length and difficulty of the text will vary depending on lesson purpose, student facility in using the process, and other learner characteristics. The process comprises three steps; each step must be followed as prescribed by the developers if the desired outcomes are to be realized (Swicegood & Parsons, 1989, p. 6).

1. The teacher instructs students to summarize the selected text and to generate questions about what they have read. To scaffold this step, the teacher poses focusing questions and prompts students to talk about the details of the selection, to make inferences, and to predict what is likely to occur next.

2. During the early stages of learning the process, the teacher serves as a model and coaches students in formulating good questions. She may provide verbal cues and prompts to assist students in framing quality questions (e.g., *Would you like to have the main character as a friend? Why or why not?*). The teacher is careful to frame questions that are at an appropriate level of difficulty to allow students to develop their confidence in thinking and speaking.

   As students become more expert in using the process, the teacher begins to transfer more control to them. He designates a student to serve as "questioner." During the more mature phases of use, the teacher functions solely as a coach. He listens carefully to questions and responses, focusing particularly upon students' thinking and reasoning skills. He intervenes only when needed to scaffold the learning of an individual student or to move the group to a higher level of thinking.

3. Throughout the process, all students are expected to pose questions to clarify their own understandings of the text. This might involve asking for the meaning of a vocabulary word or requesting additional information from a student who has answered a question. Although the developers of the reciprocal teaching process do not explicitly mention the use of wait times in the execution of reciprocal questioning, we believe that wait times add value to the learning that occurs through this process.

The research base related to reciprocal teaching is extensive. The process works with K–16 students and can be adapted to any content area wherein comprehension is a goal. What's nonnegotiable in the use of this process is teacher buy-in: In order for the process to work, the teacher using it needs to believe that collaborative discourse contributes to student learning and achievement (Palincsar & Brown, 1984).

Thinking Through QQ: What are your experiences, if any, in using think-alouds and similar strategies with students? How might you apply think-alouds and reciprocal teaching strategies with your students?

Graphic Organizers and Thinking Routines

Marzano (Marzano, Pickering, & Pollock, 2001) identifies nonlinguistic representations as one of the nine instructional strategies that work (p. 76). A favorite of teachers and students, graphic organizers, a particular subset of this strategy, are potent ways of making student thinking and responding visible. Teachers can employ these devices to record and display student answers to a range of question types. Marzano found that graphic organizers are particularly useful in displaying six types of patterns.

Given that pattern recognition is one of the most basic (and frequently tested) thinking skills, we can make a strong argument for putting graphic organizers to work in tandem with quality questions. The six pattern types identified by Marzano (Marzano et al., 2001) are (1) descriptive, (2) time sequence, (3) cause-and-effect, (4) episode, (5) generalization/principle, and (6) concept pattern (pp. 77–80). For each of these pattern types, Marzano offers visuals with which most teachers are familiar.

We find particular value in using these graphic organizers in both whole-class and collaborative settings. In a teacher-directed, whole-class setting, the teacher can pose a question designed to produce outcomes related to one of the six identified patterns. As students respond, the teacher (or a student) records responses on a whiteboard or SMART Board. This supports visual learning by helping students "see" patterns emerge.

Consider the following example: An American History teacher poses the following question to his middle school students: *Many 19th-century Americans pulled up their stakes, leaving family and friends behind, to join the westward expansion. What factors contributed to individuals' decisions to start over again in an unknown territory?* As students begin offering responses, the teacher asks them to record their individual responses on the class SMART Board. The following pattern emerges (Figure 3.9). As a student offers a new response, the teacher asks, *Where would you*

Figure 3.9   Cause-and-Effect Graphic Organizer

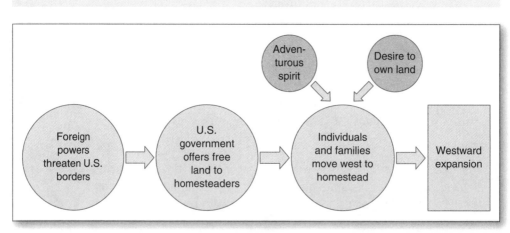

place this in our cause-and-effect chain? What is its relationship to the other ideas we have in our cause-and-effect organizer?

Currently, there are many sources for training in the use of graphic organizers, including commercial companies, such as Thinking Maps™. Often, every teacher in a school attends such training, and students begin to develop similar frames for thinking across all disciplines. Additionally, hundreds of books, journal articles, web-based resources, and consultants provide assistance to educators in systematic use of these learning tools. These kinds of tools can be powerful supports for student thinking. Their value, however, is directly related to the quality of questions a teacher crafts for use in generating input for the visuals.

Thinking Strategies

A major theme running throughout this book is the development of student responsibility and ownership for their learning. Direct connections are made between identified teacher questioning behaviors and student cognitive and metacognitive outcomes. Quality questioning is effective to the extent that it produces these outcomes for students. In addition to modeling quality questioning, teachers can provide students with tools, strategies, frameworks, and models that assist them in making their own cognitive operations visible.

Teachers typically talk about different kinds of thinking by reference to some hierarchical ordering. This is probably due to the influence of Bloom's Taxonomy (Bloom, 1956) on the categorization of thinking. Students of thinking, however, are more likely to differentiate among different types or kinds of thinking and to focus less on hierarchies. The three most common categories in the literature of thinking are decision making, conceptualizing, and problem solving (Swartz et al., 2008, p. 14). The literature is replete with models and frameworks for use in strengthening each of these types of student thinking. The most useful of these are particular to specific disciplines, for example, mathematics, science, history, literature, and the like. Because these are so readily accessible online, we do not include examples here. However, a teacher who desires to provide her students with a repertoire of tools for thinking will select models appropriate to her content area and to her students' age and maturity. Students can use these tools and schemata to map the mental steps they use in addressing problems or making decisions or in grappling with concepts.

Likewise, students benefit when provided with models to map their metacognitive activities. One field of metacognitive study is self-regulation, which is defined as "the self-directive learning process through which learners transform their mental abilities into academic skills" (Zimmerman, 1998, p. 2). Thought leaders in this field emphasize that self-regulation is neither an academic skill (such as reading proficiency) nor a mental ability (such as intelligence). Further, they agree about two important features of self-regulation: (1) Students can learn self-regulation skills, thereby, making associated metacognitive processes visible and more accessible to them, and (2) self-regulation leads to higher levels of performance (Ritchhart & Perkins, 2005; Zimmerman, 1998).

Self-regulation, like other branches of strategic thinking, engages students at three critical points in learning: (1) before, (2) during, and (3) after. For example, Zimmerman (1998) presents self-regulation as a cycle composed of three phases: (1) forethought, (2) performance, and (3) self-reflection (pp. 2–3).

Forethought occurs prior to the beginning of a learning cycle and engages students in the setting of goals and the planning of learning strategies. Essentially, the student translates learning objectives into personal learning goals or targets and decides upon learning strategies that will assist his reaching these targets. For example, a student might decide to use graphic organizers to summarize his understanding of major concepts. In a quality questioning classroom, we hope he will choose to formulate questions about the reading that can be posed to the teacher and classmates— and will adopt active and critical listening behaviors. Like other components of self-regulation, the activities associated with forethought are essential to students' use of formative feedback, which is the focus of Chapter 4.

The performance cycle, which occurs when learning goes live, involves attention focusing, self-instruction/imagery, and self-monitoring. Attention focusing engages the learner in filtering out distractions and staying focused on the learning goal. Self-instruction relates to a learner's ability to engage in self-talk during a learning task. The purpose of think-alouds and reciprocal teaching, discussed earlier in this chapter, is to strengthen student self-instruction. Self-monitoring occurs as the student reflects on progress toward meeting the learning goal. In a quality questioning classroom, students can mark their progress by seeking and processing formative feedback from both their teacher and their classmates.

Zimmerman (1998) refers to the third phase of his learning cycle as self-reflection. We call it simply student reflection, and we agree with Zimmerman that students benefit from conducting self-assessments at the end of lessons or units of study. Self-assessment or self-evaluation is equally as important as teacher evaluation in pointing to future directions for student learning. Reflection also enables students to think about what contributed to their success (or lack thereof) in learning. Research findings reveal that "self-regulated learners tend to attribute failures to correctable causes and attribute success to personal competence" (Zimmerman, p. 5).

Thinking Through QQ: Anderson and Krathwohl (2001) write that metacognitive knowledge "consists of knowledge about one's personal learning and thinking, self-assessment and self-monitoring strategies, and other strategic knowledge" (p. 45). In what ways do you think you can assist your students in developing their metacognitive knowledge?

CONNECTIONS: DEVELOPING LEARNER CAPACITY

Almost all learning occurs in a complex social environment, and learning is hard to understand if one thinks of it as a mental process occurring within the head of an isolated learner.

—R. Keith Sawyer (2009, p. 9)

Teachers' focus on strengthening thinking-to-learn behaviors involves a set of interrelated processes. Chapter 3 has focused on four processes: (1) expect thoughtful responses, (2) afford time for thinking, (3) scaffold thinking and responding, and (4) make thinking visible. Each of these makes individual contributions to the supporting and scaffolding of student thinking and learning. When we are able to incorporate all four of these components into our routine practice, they interact one with another in a synergistic manner—producing powerful learning for our students. They also add value to our featured areas of learner capacity—metacognition, engagement, and self-efficacy.

Student Metacognition

- **What am I seeking to learn or be able to do?** When we expect thoughtful responses and provide think time for our students, we communicate our expectation that their learning be personal, authentic, and embedded in their prior knowledge. This enables them to formulate learning goals that have personal meaning to them— not goals that merely mimic or conform to teacher-formulated goals. Additionally, when we assist students in making learning and thinking visible, we help them clarify the *what* and *how* of their learning. Providing a frame for "thinking about thinking" supports this important metacognitive component.
- **What do I currently know or think about the topic? Is it accurate?** Scaffolding is a strategy intended to support student responses to this question by helping students figure out a subject or problem. Teacher cues, prompts, and use of graphic organizers surface student thinking and enable the students to test this thinking publicly, to reflect, and to make adjustments.
- **How will I make personal meaning of this content?** All of the teacher behaviors presented in Chapter 3 promote personal meaning making. In fact, they rest on teacher beliefs that deep and long-lasting learning occurs only when students have opportunities to

construct meaning by relating new knowledge to what they already know. Affording students practice in thinking through the relationship between new and existing knowledge assists them in developing a lifelong thinking strategy.

- **How am I monitoring my learning and progress?** Students need time and structures to engage in effective monitoring and self-regulation. Most researchers in this field agree that teachers should provide such support before, during, and after a lesson. When teachers model and embrace the value of monitoring, they also provide opportunities for students to reflect on their own learning, which is a condition for ongoing monitoring.

- **To what extent am I developing response-ability?** Teachers and students can use the norms presented in Chapter 3 to begin answering this question. These norms are timeless and can continue to support student thinking and learning long after students have graduated from the classrooms in which they practice them.

- **What have I learned? How can I take my learning to the next level?** Student answers to these queries are much more meaningful than test grades or other formal assessments provided by teachers or other external assessors. This is the component of metacognitive processing that feeds into the motivation and desire for ongoing, independent learning.

Student Engagement

Do you still have the visual image of the instructional core in your mind? If so, your primary focus is probably on the relationship between teacher and students. Teacher expectations and active scaffolding directly involve students in classroom interactions. Each set of strategies presented in Chapter 3 engages teachers in assisting students in using their minds well. These strategies go far beyond the ritual engagement about which Phil Schlechty (2002) writes—the type of engagement in which students comply or conform to what they perceive to be appropriate going-to-school behaviors.

When teachers scaffold and make learning visible, they engage students cognitively and metacognitively. Not only are students engaged in interacting with the teacher and their classmates; they are also interacting around the content or curriculum to be studied in ways that will make it meaningful to them. Strategies such as graphic organizers serve to activate thinking about content.

Student Self-Efficacy

When students learn by doing their own thinking, their beliefs in their ability to control the outcome of their learning become more positive.

Consider the following situations and how they impact students' beliefs about their self-efficacy.

- José used to sit quietly while other students "parroted" the answers they thought the teachers wanted. However, Mr. Williams, his new sixth-grade teacher, is very clear that he wants students to answer with their own thoughts—not try to read his mind. So José is now offering his ideas, which Mr. Williams sometimes singles out as being particularly insightful.
- Bobby is a student who used to be still thinking about his answer as half of his classmates were waving their hands in the air, ready to respond to the question. Then his teacher implemented Wait Times 1 and 2. Now Bobby has time to think of his answer—and his teacher often calls on him to respond.
- Keisha is a visual learner, but since middle school, she has struggled to learn through teacher lecture and worksheets. This year her English teacher is using a range of graphic organizers to record and illustrate student thinking and responses. Keisha feels as if learning has come alive in this classroom.

These are but a few examples of the power of scaffolding to enhance self-efficacy. As you may recall, self-efficacy is associated with self-regulation, which can lead to improved performance.

Teachers offer many gifts to students. In our view, there is none more special than the gift that awakens students to their own potential and capacity to control their learning and destiny in life.

4

Use Formative Feedback

How Can Questioning Serve as
Formative Assessment and Feedback
to Advance Student Learning?

FOCUS QUESTIONS

1. What dimensions of quality questioning make it a powerful formative assessment?

2. How can teachers and students use student responses to identify gaps between current and required knowledge and skills?

3. What are the qualities of effective formative feedback?

4. How can students self-assess and work together to monitor their progress in learning?

All of assessment relates to questioning. In asking students to identify, explain, or demonstrate what they know, the teacher can identify gaps, misinformation, and misuse of knowledge.

—Laura Greenstein (2010, p. 82)

Formative assessment and feedback dramatically impact student learning. Rick Stiggins (Stiggins, Arter, Chappuis, & Chappuis, 2006) writes that "the effect of assessment *for* learning on student achievement is some four to five times greater than the effect of reduced class size. . . . Few interventions in education come close to having the same level of impact as assessment *for* learning" (p. 37). Black and Wiliam (1998a), having conducted an extensive review of studies on the topic, conclude that effective use of formative assessment produces student gains "among the largest ever reported for educational interventions" (p. 61). These and other thought leaders distinguish formative assessment, or assessment *for* learning, from summative assessment, or assessment *of* learning. And they agree that quality questioning is a primary strategy for executing this vital instructional practice (Black & Wiliam, 1998a; Fisher & Frey, 2007; Heritage, 2010; Moss & Brookhart, 2009). Simply stated, quality questioning achieves its highest purposes when put to the service of formative assessment, a key component of the learning cycle.

> Formative assessment is a process that takes place continuously during the course of teaching and learning to provide teachers and students with feedback to close the gap between learning and desired goals.
>
> —Heritage (2010, p. 10)

Questioning is the only type of assessment that can operate "continuously during the course of teaching and learning to provide teachers and students with feedback" (Heritage, 2010, p. 10). This is because questions and answers are naturally occurring parts of any lesson or learning cycle; they are not interruptions or appendages. Teachers can move seamlessly from presenting content to questioning; students can transition from attending to a teacher's delivery of instruction to responding to or asking a question. These characteristics of the questioning process qualify it as the "foot soldier" of formative assessment— operating in real time in the classroom and adapting to different contexts and circumstances.

In too many classrooms, neither teachers nor students are realizing the potential of questioning as formative assessment. Teachers pose questions, students answer, and teachers evaluate; however, these exchanges are more rituals than generators of rich data sources. Why do so many of these interactions miss the mark? First, teachers fail to systematically calibrate questions with established standards and learning goals. Further, neither teachers nor students routinely analyze student responses to identify gaps between students' existing knowledge and skills and expected learning outcomes. Nor do teachers typically provide students formative feedback when they offer incorrect or incomplete responses; rather, they evaluate responses as to their correctness and move on to their next question. Finally, teachers do not consistently view student responses as feedback to use in decision making about next steps for instruction.

How can teachers transform traditional usage of questioning into a game changer in the learning process? The challenges are to (1) ask questions that will generate data that demonstrate where students are in their progress toward learning goals (i.e., identify the gaps), (2) use student answers as feedback to inform instruction that will close identified gaps, and (3) communicate this feedback to students in ways that will enable them to modify learning strategies and correct misunderstandings.

In this chapter, we make the case that the dimensions of quality questioning, discussed earlier in the book, also serve the purposes of formative assessment. In fact, when done most effectively, quality questioning is indistinguishable from formative assessment. This chapter is organized around teacher behaviors that effectively employ quality questioning as a game-changing tool for formative assessment:

- Employ questions to assess student progress toward learning goals.
- Identify gaps, if any, between current and expected knowledge and skills.
- Provide feedback to students.
- Use feedback to inform instruction.

Thinking Through QQ: To what extent do you intentionally and systematically use questioning to facilitate formative assessment and feedback to support students learning? How do you assess your current use of these practices?

EMPLOY QUESTIONS TO ASSESS STUDENT PROGRESS TOWARD LEARNING GOALS

All of the elements of quality questions discussed in Chapter 2 apply to questioning as formative assessment. For teachers and students to assess knowledge and performance accurately, questions need to be aligned with specific learning targets that are clear to students. The questions need to be appropriately challenging for students—not too easy and not too difficult. Most frequently, teachers will want to pose questions that go beyond simple recall, asking students to demonstrate understanding through application of knowledge in a different context (i.e., transfer), to explain the process of their thinking, or to analyze and summarize information. More specifically, questioning becomes a highly productive vehicle for formative assessment and feedback when teachers adopt the behaviors associated with the first stage of the Framework for Thinking Through Quality Questioning, frame quality questions, and when students themselves ask questions that engage them in self-assessment.

Frame Questions That Assess Student Progress Toward Learning Goals

You may recall that the first behavior associated with framing quality questions is to *determine the content focus*. We have underscored the importance of focusing the content of a question on learning goals derived from state standards. In turn, the first criterion for productive formative assessments is that teachers determine learning goals and criteria for success, communicate these to students, and align assessments with these goals. When teachers communicate learning goals, students can then translate them into learning targets as they ask themselves, *What am I seeking to learn or be able to do?* Then, when teachers ask questions that align with learning targets, students will understand the relevance of the teacher's questions to their own learning.

By aligning questions with identified instructional goals, teachers are better able to be clear about the acceptable parameters of student answers. When teachers ask simple remember questions, students need only provide the requisite knowledge. However, questions above the remember level call for both requisite knowledge and also thinking skills. To prepare for the delivery of effective feedback, it is important for teachers to figure out exactly what the thinking elicited by a question should sound like. This will enable the teacher to provide feedback related to both knowledge and thinking skills—or to develop a rubric or criteria for an acceptable answer that can be used by students for self-assessment or by groups of students in peer assessment. Later in this chapter, we offer suggestions for forming and delivering feedback on thinking.

Another consideration in the design of a quality question is the social context in which it will be delivered. In Chapter 2, we differentiated among questions formulated for delivery by the teacher to one or more students, those designed by the teacher for use in cooperative or collaborative groups, and those crafted for response and self-assessment by students working independently. Typically, we think of teachers asking assessment questions to individuals or groups of students. However, self-assessment and peer assessments are key components of formative assessment, and research tells us that self-assessment is one of the most effective tools for learning. This makes it critical for teachers to be intentional in formulating questions that are appropriate for use in independent and group contexts for learning. We will have more to say about student self-assessment later in this section.

Finally, if a question is to yield an accurate assessment of what a student knows and can do, the student must understand what the question is asking. A quality question must be clear and succinct, thereby communicating to students both the knowledge and the thinking requirements of an acceptable response.

Creating quality questions that will assess student progress toward a learning goal is difficult work. Several positive benefits accrue to teachers who practice this discipline. First, the act of formulating questions as a part of the lesson planning process helps teachers become clearer in their own minds about learning goals and how they can be measured. One study shows that after involvement in a yearlong project to develop skills in formative assessment, teachers reported spending more time planning than grading. "By thinking more carefully about the questions they ask in class, teachers can check on students' understanding while the students are still in class rather than after they have left, as is the case with grading" (Leahy, Lyon, Thompson, & Wiliam, 2005, p. 21).

Teachers' collaborative creation of questions is powerful. As teachers work in grade-level or disciplinary teams, they talk together about standards and develop or examine learning goals that they use to focus quality questions. Thinking with colleagues to conceptualize questions increases question quality. Following the use of these focus questions in their classrooms, teachers bring student response data back to team meetings where they share and compare data and reflect together about where students are in their learning. Teachers consider next steps in instruction. They also reflect on the value of the questions they designed and tweak them, if appropriate, for use with future students.

Thinking Through QQ: Reflect on the characteristics of quality questions that make them particularly appropriate for formative assessment. Do you consciously frame questions with the intent of using them as formative assessments? Do your students know that questioning in your classroom is for this purpose?

Promote Student Self-Assessment

While teacher questions are essential vehicles in the formative assessment of student learning, proactive student self-assessments are no less important. Students who are developing their metacognitive and self-regulatory skills ask themselves these kinds of questions: *Do I know the answer to this question? Am I confident of my answer? Can I defend my answer with examples and with logical reasoning? Do I think more than one answer is possible? Do I understand the level of thinking that is required—and, am I sure that my answer meets the standard for that level of thinking? If I don't know the answer, or if I am unsure what the question is asking, what question will I ask to find out?* If students are to pose such questions, teachers must afford them time for this purpose.

Most of these self-assessment questions occur during the pause after the teacher poses the question: Wait Time 1. In a classroom where every student is responsible to formulate an answer to every question, all the students will be considering these questions as they create their responses. If the teacher uses a cooperative-learning response format such as Think-Pair-Share before asking for whole-class responses, students have another opportunity for self-assessment—this time with a partner. As they say their answer aloud to a partner, they can reflect on the reasons behind their thinking and assess the extent to which their answer is correct. And as they listen to their partner talk, they can compare their answer: *Are we both correct? Do we believe the same thing? Why is his answer different from mine? Can both of us provide a rationale for our answers?* If time allows, they will likely give one another feedback—especially if one of the answers is incorrect.

As the teacher asks for a student to share a response to the question, Wait Time 2 provides an additional opportunity for self-assessment. For the student who is called on to answer, thinking and self-assessment continue during the silence that follows her response. During this silence, she may be asking herself, *Is this answer correct? Do I have anything else to say that would more clearly articulate my position? Would examples be more persuasive? Do I want to pose an alternative or ask a question to clarify my thinking? Do I feel confident about my answer? Have I answered at the appropriate cognitive level?*

In our experience, when students don't know about Wait Time 2 and its purpose of promoting thinking, the first thought that comes into their minds during the silence that follows their response is, *Well, my answer isn't correct or the teacher would have let me know.* In traditional classrooms, where students have not learned the norm of using time to think about their answers, students are answering to give the teacher's answer. They have done all the thinking they are going to do; now, it is time for the teacher to let them know if they are correct or incorrect. This all-too-common norm of answering for the teacher does not promote self-assessment or thoughtfulness.

> Self-assessment by pupils, far from being a luxury, is in fact an essential component of formative assessment.
>
> —Black & Wiliam (1998b, p. 143)

What about the student who is not called on? As he listens to his fellow student respond, he assesses his thinking. During the silence, he might ask, *Do I agree with that? Do I have anything to add? Do I disagree? If so, can I provide a clear rationale for my answer? Is it possible that both answers are correct? What questions could I ask to better understand her response?*

During Wait Time 2, as the students are thinking, the teacher is formulating appropriate feedback. Also, one of the nonresponding students may chime in: *I was thinking the same thing. But I had a different reason for my answer.* The discussion may continue as other students add their thoughts, giving one another feedback and simultaneously assessing their thinking. The teacher enters this discussion to recognize and build on correct answers, to pose additional questions, or to ask for evidence—modeling for students thoughtful and respectful ways to engage in discussion. The teacher may also provide feedback regarding misconceptions or wrong answers as they occur.

In many classes, where teachers don't know about or forget to use Wait Time 2 in an intentional, nonthreatening way, the teacher evaluates the answer, and the class moves on—long before the process of self-assessment has occurred. Students speak to the teacher, not to one another, and the ritual continues. The consistent use of wait time actually extends student thinking and self-assessment while teacher reactions to student responses tend to stifle thinking.

Thinking Through QQ: What can you do to encourage your students to use every classroom question as an opportunity for self-assessment? Would your students be surprised to learn that they have a responsibility to monitor their learning?

When students are active in the assessment process, rather than passive recipients of assessment, they take more responsibility for their learning and are more motivated to learn. They essentially own the learning and have an important part in assessing the accuracy of their responses. In classrooms where formative assessment is intentionally used, students understand assessment to be a part of the learning process. They further understand that the role of their teachers is to help them develop responsibility to think through and to assess their answers.

How do students learn to self-assess? Some students come to school with this skill; others require more explicit instruction. All can benefit from opportunities to reflect on what they have learned and how they are learning. Additionally, they develop insights as they talk about their learning processes and listen to other students talk about theirs. Teachers can provide specific cues to elicit other students' thinking. After a student responds, the teacher may inquire, *Show me a thumbs up if you agree,* and call on one of those students to explain why the answer is correct. Alternately, after a student gives a correct answer, the teacher may ask a follow-up question (*Can you explain how you arrived at that answer?*) to have the student explicitly talk about her thinking to let

Students should be taught to ask questions about their own work and revise their learning as a result of reflection—in effect, to conduct their own formative assessment. When students . . . have opportunities to assess their own and others' learning . . . there is a transfer of power from teacher to learner. On the other hand, when formative feedback is "owned" entirely by the teacher, the power of the learner in the classroom is diminished, and the development of active and independent learning is inhibited.

—Pellegrino, Chudowsky, & Glaser (2001, p. 237)

other students hear the process of thinking. All of these tools contribute to student self-assessment.

Structure Peer Assessment

Black and his fellow researchers (2003) found that "in practice, peer assessment turns out to be an important complement and may even be a prior requirement for self-assessment" (p. 52). These researchers offer three compelling reasons for this phenomenon: (1) Students tend to be more motivated and work more carefully when they know their peers will be assessing their work, (2) students better understand peer suggestions because they are speaking their language, and (3) the teacher is more likely to pay attention to feedback received from a group than to feedback from a single student.

If peer assessments are to be valid and valuable, students need to have a common set of criteria to use as they assess their peers. Once again, rubrics are valuable tools for students seeking to understand the success criteria associated with a given learning target. Most often, peer assessments occur in the context of collaborative groups. Teachers can frame questions for use by groups in exploring a given topic and provide the groups with a rubric by which to assess their responses.

Protocols for critical-friend reviews provide structure and scaffolding for peer assessors. In an elementary school outside of Memphis, Tennessee, we recently watched one such protocol in action. In groups of four, students listened as their peers read a story or essay they had written. In each group, two students read their stories, and the other two asked questions and provided positive and constructive feedback to the readers. Students used a modified version of the state writing rubric in the formulation of their feedback. Additionally, they made suggestions about ways the writing might be improved. We witnessed firsthand the way this reflective activity helped students begin to write to please themselves, rather than their teachers. They began to establish their goals for good writing, and they knew when they had achieved mastery and when they needed improvement. It was easier for students to learn the self-assessment process by first applying it to other students' stories. After all, it is easier to recognize a need for improvement in others' work than in your own (Leahy et al., 2005, p. 23). The skill of analysis and assessment transferred to their own writing and was a transformative experience in the learning lives of these children.

IDENTIFY GAPS, IF ANY, BETWEEN CURRENT AND EXPECTED KNOWLEDGE AND SKILLS

Here's the game changer! The formulation and delivery of quality questions that elicit thoughtful and thorough student answers is only the tip-off. Once a student answer is on the floor, the real game begins. The teacher's role is to analyze student answers by comparing embedded knowledge and thinking to the expected student response, which is aligned with success criteria. During this process, the teacher identifies both (1) what the student knows and can do and (2) discrepancies, if any, between the actual and desired level of student knowledge and skill. Any identified discrepancy between the two constitutes a learning gap. And as students become more adept as self-assessors, they assume ever greater responsibility in identifying these gaps for themselves. Essential to formulation of effective feedback is determining whether a learning gap exists and, if so, what it entails. Figure 4.1 displays the component parts of questioning as formative assessment and feedback and the relationships of the components one to another.

As previously stated, the learning gap expresses the relationship between a student's current knowledge and skills and those required to attain a specified learning target. Margaret Heritage (2010), a well-known

Figure 4.1 Relationship of Learning Gap to Question, Response, and Feedback

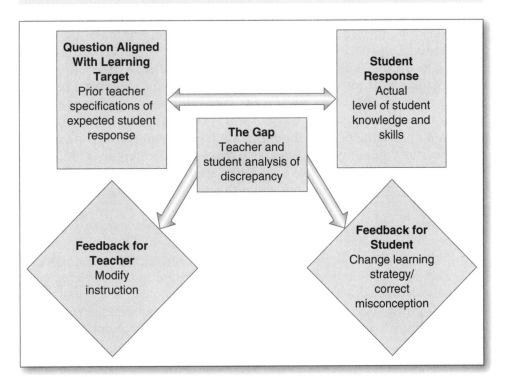

student of formative assessment, writes, "Students who are learning something new should have a gap, otherwise learning is not advancing" (p. 12). She further contends that "interpreting the evidence from formative assessment is key to identifying the gap" (p. 13). This speaks to the most appropriate level of challenge or difficulty for quality questions. We mentioned in earlier chapters that quality questions challenge students within their zone of proximal development, or ZPD. This means that the learning gap generated by a question for any given student should be within that student's ZPD. Otherwise, the student, lacking adequate prior knowledge and skills on which to build, would be frustrated and unable to use any formative feedback provided.

Formative feedback to students must achieve two ends: (1) promote the learner's perception or understanding of the gap between his current understanding (as embodied in his response to a question) and the desired level of understanding, and (2) guide and stimulate the student to take actions to close the identified gap. As Black and colleagues (2003) argue, "The learner first has to understand the evidence about this gap and then take action on the basis of that evidence" (p. 14). These authors do not diminish the teacher's role in assisting the learner in understanding the gap, but they maintain that "the learning has to be done by the student. It would be a mistake to regard the student as a passive recipient of any call to action" (p. 14).

The process required to identify a particular student's learning gap requires the teacher to execute higher-order thinking in real time during a dynamic classroom interaction. If the teacher is to facilitate the previous two end goals of formative feedback, she must complete the analysis required to identify this gap. And for this analysis, she must be crystal clear about the expected student response and the student's current level of knowledge and skills (embodied in his answer). Recall that in Chapter 3 we provided a planning template for use in outlining the critical parameters of an acceptable response and for thinking about other answers that students might offer to a given question. This tool can greatly enhance a teacher's ability to conduct the type of analysis required to determine a given learning gap. Figure 4.2 can be used as a quick reference reminder to listen actively and carefully to a student's answer for the purpose of identifying the student's current understanding or skill level regarding thinking. Sometimes teachers need to check with a student to ensure that they understand what the student is attempting to express. Asking clarifying questions of the student can assist teachers in verifying their interpretation of a student's answer. Only when the teacher is clear regarding the expected response and the thinking behind the actual response can she engage in the analysis that leads to identification of the gap.

During this and subsequent stages of the gap-identification process, it is the teacher who is challenged to think: to analyze the student's answer in order to break it into its constituent parts, to compare and contrast the answer to the expected response, to identify aspects of the student's answer

Figure 4.2 Process for Determining Student Learning Gap

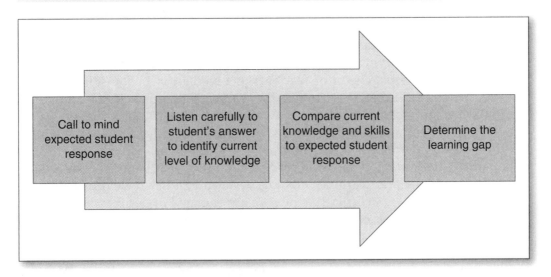

that are correct and can be extended, to isolate errors in student knowledge and thinking (if any) to be able to provide appropriate assistance through scaffolding or assignment of supplemental learning tasks, and to determine how to communicate this gap to the student. Wait Time 2 provides time for teachers to engage in this challenging thinking. This analysis is critical if the teacher is to support the student in understanding the gap and deciding how to close it. The teacher either provides this support directly by offering direct feedback to students or indirectly by scaffolding students in the self-assessment that leads to the identification of the gap and determination of their own next moves. The most effective coaches—and teachers—oftentimes choose the latter course as they seek to develop these capacities in their students so that they themselves can make crucial decisions about their learning and performance as they seek to reach goals.

Thinking Through QQ: What is your experience in identifying student learning gaps? Have you applied this discipline to the analysis of student answers to your oral questions? If so, with what results?

PROVIDE FEEDBACK TO STUDENTS

Formative feedback comes only after we (1) frame and ask questions that generate evidence about student learning and (2) analyze the student answer to identify learning gaps. As emphasized earlier, we cannot

jump directly from the asking of a question to the provision of feedback—
if the feedback is to be truly formative. Yet most of us are products of
classrooms in which teachers asked questions and evaluated their correctness in a one-two punch fashion—omitting the rigorous step of comparing the student answer to an optimal expected response for the
purpose of identifying that gap. Our hypothesis is that the traditional
approach to the provision of feedback evolved from behaviorism and
operant conditioning that touted the value of positive and negative
reinforcement to mold behavior. Academic learning, however, is not
comparable to maze-running, and simple evaluative feedback does not
promote standards-based learning.

Rich, descriptive, data-based feedback, on the other hand, is a powerful driver of complex learning. All of us perform best when we receive this
type of feedback—particularly when we are engaged in perfecting a complex task. Regardless of the situation—whether we watch ourselves in the
gym mirror to adjust our physical movements during a workout, "taste
test" when preparing a meal, have a friend give feedback on a resume, or
discover a discrepancy between the bank statement and our checkbook—
our performance is enhanced by feedback.

For feedback to be effective and meaningful to the learner, however,
the person receiving it must be clear about what constitutes exemplary (or
at least adequate) performance. For example, consider the following:
bending the knees slightly when lifting weights, preparing tasty food that
prompts guests to ask for the recipe, matching one's professional experience to the known requirements of a job opening, or balancing a checkbook. Feedback is meaningless unless one knows what one is aiming to
achieve. This is true for athletes, cooks, job seekers, and people going
about their everyday business. It's also true for students who require criteria for success to assess their performance. Sometimes teachers embed
these in rubrics; other times they provide exemplars. You may wish to
review Figure 2.1, which establishes criteria for student responses to quality questions.

Thinking Through QQ: What type of feedback did you receive from your
teachers when you were a student? When did you first experience formative feedback as a learner?

In any endeavor, feedback is particularly important for those who are
developing new skills. Think of the feedback that was required when you
were a novice driver. You needed to constantly check your position on the
road, test the play in the steering wheel, look in the rear-view mirror, esti-
mate the distance between your car and the one in front of you, and apply

just the right amount of pressure to the gas pedal or the brakes. These are things that experienced drivers do without much thought. Similarly, think back to your first year of teaching! Constantly, you wanted feedback: *What can I do to capture my students' attention? What would be a better strategy for helping them learn how to read critically?* How am I doing? was the continual refrain in your mind. Even as experienced teachers, when faced with something new—a new curriculum, new teaching strategies, or a shift in the demographics of our student population—we become less certain of our performance, and we need increased feedback to help us develop skills and confidence.

It is the same for students. As they learn new things, face uncertainty as learners, or confront failure, they require feedback to optimize their performance. As they become more skilled—in the process of learning, in a certain unit of study, or in a particular discipline—students become more confident and are more able to assess their own performance and to adjust their ideas or behaviors to make improvements.

> Good feedback causes thinking.
>
> —Stiggins et al. (2006, p. 279)

Characteristics of Effective Formative Feedback

Thus far in this chapter, we have attempted to create a shared understanding regarding the *what* and the *why* of formative feedback. We have further sought to underscore the importance of (1) basing feedback upon evidence regarding an identified learning gap and (2) incorporating strategies for closing that gap into the feedback. But how does one go about formulating the actual feedback statement itself? Figure 4.3 provides six attributes of effective and ineffective formative feedback, and it is a helpful springboard for thinking about how to craft feedback statements that promote student thinking and learning.

Although these characteristics can be applied to any type of feedback—written or oral—we are interested in their implications for oral feedback that follows a student's answer to a classroom question posed by the teacher. The quick-reference information in Figure 4.3 can assist a teacher in formulating feedback on the spot during the heat of the teaching-learning process.

Describe a student's status in relation to the learning target; give specific and descriptive examples. Formative feedback answers the question *Where are you in relationship to the learning target?* This is the question that helps a student identify where she is compared with where she hopes to be. Effective feedback is not evaluative; that is to say, formative feedback does not merely convey whether a response is correct. Rather, it is descriptive, meaning it refers specifically to some component of the student's answer. *Your comment indicates that you considered the perspectives of both of the major*

Figure 4.3   Characteristics of Effective and Ineffective Formative Feedback

Effective Feedback	Ineffective Feedback
Describes a student's status in relationship to the learning target; gives specific and descriptive examples	Is evaluative and may be vague or general
Connects to criteria that have been previously communicated to students or that students have helped to develop	Is based on teacher discretion; is not linked to specific criteria
Involves students actively	Is directed and controlled by the teacher
Uses words carefully in a helpful, positive tone	May be misinterpreted or taken as criticism
Includes suggestions for how to improve	Provides no suggestions for ways to improve
Is timely	Is delivered too late to make a difference

characters provides information about what the student did that met established criteria. Evaluative comments such as *Good thinking* or *This is an incomplete response* are so general that they don't help students know what part of their response is acceptable or what they need to do to improve. Probes can help both the teacher and the student learn more about the student's progress toward a learning goal. For example, if a teacher says, *Tell me how you verified the reliability of the information that came from the Internet*, both can learn something about the student's skill in identifying valid sources.

In a study of third-grade classrooms, the majority of positive teacher feedback statements were vague and lacking in specific examples. *Very good* was a typical teacher comment in response to a student answer. In sixth-grade math classes, the same trend was found. This type of response does not constitute effective feedback. Also, researchers have discovered that when teachers included specific feedback with examples of what students did correctly, student self-efficacy improved (Huebner, 2009, p. 91).

Connect to criteria that have been previously communicated to students or that students have helped to develop. Teachers who understand the importance of feedback will have helped students as they translated the learning target into student-friendly words. By knowing the learning targets, students understand the criteria by which their responses will be assessed; this information positively impacts student achievement (Marzano, 2007, p. 104).

The practice of aligning questions and resultant feedback with learning targets is essential if we want feedback to result in improved student performance. Unfortunately, the lack of well-defined learning targets makes this practice uncommon in schools. For example, if a teacher focuses questions and feedback on discrete facts or bits of knowledge, students may be able to regurgitate the facts but be unable to make connections between and among disparate facts. Thus, opportunities for true learning are lost. *What was the intended learning target? What type of thinking or cognitive processing is required to attain this target?* If students never receive feedback on their thinking or analytic skills, they are unlikely to improve in this area.

Involve students actively. Quality questioning—whether used during class recitations or discussions—engages students in thinking. Questioning can also be used in conjunction with students' completion of a written assignment. Questions are an ideal way to prompt student reflection and thinking about written work products. For example, if a student has produced a pie chart to demonstrate an answer to a social studies question, a teacher might help the student think about alternatives by asking, *How else could you display the data?* Once the student responds or produces an alternative illustration, the teacher might continue, *Which of these explains the data better? Which would be easier to understand, and why?* The most powerful questions engage students in self-assessment. For example, when a teacher asks a student to rethink the question and/or reflect on his answer, the teacher is inviting the student to self-assess and self-correct. We should aspire to this type of student involvement in assessment and feedback.

Use words carefully in a helpful, positive tone. Teachers know the value of using words that demonstrate respect, never belittling students or using sarcasm, even in a joking manner. How students interpret the feedback—not how it is intended—determines whether it will have a positive impact on achievement. When feedback is discouraging, student achievement decreases (Marzano, 2007, pp. 104–105). Monitor student nonverbals to determine if they understand and are processing your feedback. Never use false praise; most of the time, students know when teacher praise is genuine.

Include suggestions about how to improve. To be helpful to student performance, feedback needs to identify what, specifically, students did well and offer discrete suggestions as to how students can improve. "In the classroom, providing students with information about particular qualities of their work *and about what they can do to improve* is crucial for maximizing learning" (Pellegrino, Chudowsky, & Glaser, 2001, p. 8; emphasis added). Hattie (2009) describes findings from a meta-analysis by Kluger and DeNisi specific to feedback. They found that "feedback is more effective when it provides information on correct rather than incorrect responses" (p. 175). Our reading of this finding is that we are more effective when we build upon what the student knows and can do, making suggestions that will enable the student to connect suggestions for improvement to existing skills or knowledge. If we offer suggestions that seem foreign to the student because she has no background for understanding them, the feedback is likely to fall on deaf ears.

Be timely. There is universal agreement that feedback must be timely if it is to be useful; that is, the feedback should be communicated to the student as close to the student's response to a question or problem as possible—but not before three to five seconds of wait time! This is one of the reasons that classroom questioning, when effectively managed, is such a powerful type of formative assessment: The feedback following a student response can be immediate.

> *Thinking Through QQ:* Ask your students what they are doing and why. Do they understand what learning targets you are trying to help them accomplish? Do they own the learning goals? If they can articulate the learning targets, remind them that these constitute the endgame and that your feedback to them will be designed to help them meet these targets. If not, talk with them about how you might assist them in becoming more conversant with learning targets for your class.

What About Praise as Feedback?

Praise, long thought to be positive reinforcement for student performance, only rarely meets the criteria for effective feedback. Praise is an overused strategy in K–12 classrooms, and it is largely ineffective because teacher expressions of praise (e.g., *Good job! I like that. Great! You're so smart!*) are evaluative rather than descriptive. Such generic statements do not tell students what is positive or subpar about their performance, nor do they convey information about how to improve.

Further, research studies have found that praise can actually harm students' motivation and persistence with difficult tasks. Dweck (2006) reports, "Praising students' intelligence gives them a short burst of pride, followed by a long string of negative consequences" (p. 36). She found that praising effort, on the other hand, helps strengthen students' feelings of efficacy. Although it doesn't meet all of the criteria for effective feedback mentioned in Figure 4.3, praise of effort (linking what the student did with the results of the effort) is much more effective in building motivation than praise of intelligence.

Hattie (2009) identifies four areas to which feedback can be directed: (1) the task, (2) the process of learning, (3) self-regulation of learning, and (4) self (pp. 177–178). This last area— which pertains to personal characteristics of the student—is most often where praise is directed. Yet it has relatively less to do with the specific task or processes of learning used by the student. In his bestseller, *Drive*, Daniel Pink (2009) asserts that a carrots-and-sticks approach (extrinsic motivation) works against building intrinsic motivation. He cites an experiment in which students who received rewards for drawing (which they demonstrated that they enjoyed doing) actually chose to draw less frequently after receiving promised rewards for drawing. Pink contends that rewards tend to take the joy (and autonomy) out of activities; when we expect and receive tangible rewards, the task seems less fulfilling or fun. He observes that "school children who are paid to solve problems typically choose easier problems and therefore learn less" (p. 58). The take-away from this finding to the questioning arena is that gold stars, M&M's, and *Great job!* should be used sparingly.

Tailor Feedback to Match the Cognitive Level of the Question

Appropriate feedback varies depending upon the complexity and the cognitive level of the question posed. As previously argued, the assessment of a student answer to identify learning gaps and the subsequent provision of feedback is a complex cognitive task. In fact, this is the aspect of quality questioning that we personally find to be most challenging. Most of us are fairly skilled in assessing the correctness of the knowledge component of a student's answer. Hence, we are able to provide feedback to remember-level questions quickly and with relative ease. We are also able to identify knowledge gaps within higher-level questions. The real test is to offer on-the-spot feedback that focuses on the cognitive processing dimension of student responses. This is a higher-level skill for teachers, one that requires both preparation and practice.

As shown in Figure 4.4, when students are asked to respond to basic remember questions that request simple recall of facts, teachers react with an assessment as to whether the response is correct or incorrect. At the understand and apply levels, appropriate feedback is indirect; it asks students to explain their thinking and how they arrived at their answer. At the highest cognitive levels (analyze, evaluate, and create), teachers should provide feedback on the knowledge dimension but focus on student thinking. At these levels, many answers are possible, so the teacher is not looking for one correct answer. If the thinking has led the student to an incorrect answer, however, the teacher should guide the student to a correct answer.

Feedback for remember questions. Researchers have consistently found that between 60% and 80% of the questions that are asked in classrooms are at the lowest level of the Bloom Taxonomy: remember (Barnette, Walsh, Orletsky, & Sattes, 1995; Gall, 1984). For questions at the recall or remember level, feedback to a correct answer can be quite simple: *Yes, 72 is the product of 9 times 8.* Rather than giving an immediate affirmative reaction, however, teachers might withhold feedback and ask, *Who else had that answer? Show me a thumbs up if you had that answer. Tell me why you think this answer is correct (or incorrect).* In this way, other students are accountable to evaluate the responses of their peers and, as a by-product, to engage in self-assessment.

Figure 4.4   Types of Feedback Related to the Cognitive Level of the Question

Cognitive Level of Question	Type of Feedback
Remember	Let students know if the answer is correct or incorrect. Provide cues or clues to guide them to a correct answer.
Understand, Apply	Ask students to elaborate, explain their answers, or expand on their responses: *Can you give an example?* or *Say more.* Let students know if their answers are factually correct or incorrect.
Analyze, Evaluate, Create	Provide feedback on students' thinking. Say, *Help me know how you arrived at that answer,* or, *Tell me what was behind your selection of that response.* Let students know if their answers are factually correct or incorrect.

When a student's answer is not correct, before giving corrective feedback (the correct answer), ask the student to explain his thinking. You might say, *Tell me why you think that is the answer,* or, *Say more about how you came to that answer.* Sometimes it is appropriate to give simple negative feedback: *No. That is not correct.* Alternatively, teachers might choose to ask the class if others had the same (thumbs up) or different (thumbs down) answers, and then follow up by asking, *Why do you think your answer is correct?* and inviting other students to think about the answer and evaluate its correctness.

Another strategy to use when remember-level questions are incorrect is to give students the question to which their answer is correct. *If I had asked you the name of the largest city in Texas, the answer would have been Houston. But I asked you for the name of the capital city of Texas. Can you think what that might be?* If no answer is forthcoming, a teacher may choose to give cues, which may become more and more explicit in helping the student find the answer. For example, *It's a city named after a soldier who led the fight to avenge the loss at the Alamo. It's a city in the center of the state. It's where the University of Texas is located. It begins with an A.*

In no case is the use of sarcasm or criticism appropriate when a student answers incorrectly. Nor is a reaction that attempts to save face for the student, such as *Good try!* or *Let's see if Mary can help you out.* As in the case of using praise for a simple correct fact, this reaction is somewhat disingenuous. Students need to know if the answer is correct or not; they do not need to be saved from embarrassment because hopefully they will have embraced a classroom norm that values all answers—not just correct ones.

Thinking Through QQ: In most classrooms, teachers provide the correct answer when an incorrect response is given by a student. Why might it be important to provide hints so that a student can answer the question herself, rather than answering the question for the student?

Feedback for performance above the remember level. When students answer questions at cognitive levels above the remember level of the Revised Bloom Taxonomy (Anderson & Krathwohl, 2001), a different type of formative feedback is required. Even with complex questions or assignments, many of us rely on the old standby, *Good job!* or other such meaningless feedback when we could, with some effort, provide feedback that lets students know where they are in relationship to their goal and how they might continue to make progress. In Chapter 3, we offered multiple strategies for getting behind and scaffolding student thinking. You may wish to review those sections of Chapter 3 in order to reflect more deeply about how to increase your proficiency in providing feedback to higher-level questions.

Figure 4.4 distinguishes between the type of feedback you might offer to a response at the understand or apply levels and that you might provide to a student response at the analyze, evaluate, or create levels. One rule of thumb applies to feedback for student comments at all five of these levels: Ensure that your feedback focuses on both the knowledge and the cognitive processing dimensions. Too many times, we are tempted to accept a student's answer if it contains correct knowledge—even if the thinking or cognitive processing embedded in the student response is not at the intended level. In this instance, the appropriate protocol is to reinforce what is correct and then move to scaffold or otherwise assist in helping the student correct the thinking. On the other hand, we have been guilty of being so blown away by a student's thinking that we failed to provide feedback on an erroneous fact. The bottom line is this: We need to attend to both knowledge and cognitive processing dimensions as we listen to students' answers, analyze them, and determine whether learning gaps exist.

Thinking Through QQ: Teachers pose more than 50 questions in a typical hour of instruction. Such rapid-fire questions leave little room for thoughtful responses. How can we communicate to students that we, as teachers, are interested in what and how they are thinking? What strategies might you use to ask fewer questions—albeit questions that give you and students more information about their learning progress? How might you engage students in this effort?

How Can We Harness Technology in the Service of Feedback?

Technology can be used in a variety of ways to provide immediate feedback to students. Teachers and peers can use the track changes feature in Microsoft Word, for example, to comment on written products. Students can also use computer software tools to get direct feedback on grammar, spelling, and readability. Many computerized learning programs offer immediate, customized feedback that can help make learning active and fun for students of all ages and ability levels. Computer games such as Math Playground, ExploreLearning, and BrainPOP are available for a wide range of learners and content areas (Pitler, Hubbell, Kuhn, & Malenoski, 2007, pp. 51–52). Still, teachers must assure that such games are appropriately challenging for students—not too easy and not too difficult. They will also need to determine whether the feedback offered by selected games and other technology applications meet the six previously described criteria for effective feedback.

Another way to give immediate feedback to a group is to use student response systems in which every student has access to a clicker they can use to respond to teacher questions. As teachers pose questions and provide multiple-choice response options, students feed their answers into the system. Results can be shown graphically, as they are on television game shows such as *Who Wants to Be a Millionaire?* If there is only one correct answer to the questions, teachers can pose follow-up questions to hear student thinking about their choices: *I'd like to hear from someone who selected response A. I'd like to hear you explain why you believe A is correct.* If there are multiple correct answers, teachers can ask students to defend their own or another response.

Like many of the low-tech tools suggested in Resource B, web-based data collection tools such as Survey Monkey, Web Surveyor, or Pollcat allow teachers to pose questions to all students—or to a subgroup—to assess what they know. Blogs and wikis can also be used to provide feedback to students—from teachers and from other students. Other web-based tools are available to help teachers (and students) develop rubrics for lessons. Two of them are RubiStar and Rubrics for Web Lessons. Websites such as TeAchnology Web Portal for Educators include teacher-designed rubrics.

Help Students Use Feedback to Inform Their Learning

Students are more inclined to accept and use feedback in a classroom permeated by trust and respect, a classroom in which they are encouraged to engage in risk taking. In such classrooms, students and teachers alike believe that errors are not bad and can, in fact, lead to valuable lessons—an idea that is further explored in Chapter 6.

 Norm: Use mistakes as an opportunity to learn. This is a risk-free classroom.

In classrooms where students are accustomed to receiving and using feedback from their teachers, students understand that questions are posed for good reasons: to help teachers learn what and how students are thinking, to help students know what and how they themselves think, and to help other students hear different ways of thinking. Teachers need to work hard to help students understand this concept, as it is contrary to most school experiences. A norm posted in the room to encourage students to say what they think might read something like this:

 Norm: Share what you think so others can learn from you.

Formative feedback requires both teachers and students to understand that student learning is a process that takes place within each student—not a series of correct answers. The process of true learning finds students headed toward a clearly identified and attainable target, for which understandable criteria exist by which students can assess their own progress. During the learning process, students, their peers, and their teacher can all provide helpful feedback. This feedback can act as a GPS to let students know where they are in relation to mastery—but only if they become aware of how they can use feedback to guide them toward a particular educational goal or destination. Quality questioning can be used to help students think more deeply not only about the content of a lesson but also about the learning process itself. Hattie (2009), however, reports that "feedback is not often observed in classrooms despite the claims of the best teachers that they are constantly engaged in providing feedback" (p. 173).

USE FEEDBACK TO INFORM INSTRUCTION

If teachers are instrumental in ensuring that students have access to formative feedback, it is students who are the primary source of feedback to teachers. Student feedback comes through the answers they give to teacher questions and the nature and extent of the learning gaps they reveal. Student feedback also comes from the questions that students ask—particularly questions that seek clarification or direction. When teachers seek out and process these kinds of feedback from students, they are honoring student voice and conveying to students that they are partners in the teaching-learning process.

Daniel Pink (2009) asserts that in order to reach mastery, one must "seek constant, critical feedback. If you don't know how you're doing, you won't know what to improve" (p. 159). Highly effective teachers, like masters in any profession, are always looking for feedback in order to improve. Student work products and student responses to classroom questions offer teachers a rich source of feedback about how well they have facilitated student achievement of learning targets. Everything that happens in a classroom offers the potential for feedback to teachers: student contributions in discussions, student questions, small-group products—the list goes on. The difficulty lies in determining how to select the data that yield the most helpful information to inform teachers.

Imagine that a teacher wants students to learn how to use symbols to represent numerical relationships and to understand those relationships in pre-algebra. The following word problem might be used as a starting point:

Which equation represents the following statement?

There are six times as many students as teachers in the room today.

Let s = the number of students

Let t = the number of teachers

   A. $6s = t$

   B. $6t = s$

   C. $st = 6$

A problem such as this can inform a teacher—at the beginning, middle, or end of a unit—about the number of students who understand how to use symbols to represent numerical relationships. A teacher might use clickers or whiteboards to get a read on the understanding of the class as a whole. If many students select the correct answer, the teacher might ask them to share the answer they selected—and the reason for selecting that answer—with a partner.

Similarly, a teacher who wants to help students understand place value in decimals might pose a range-finding question such as *How many decimal numbers exist between 0.1 and 0.2?* (Leahy et al., 2005). If most students answer none, the teacher knows this is an area for which direct instruction, use of manipulatives, and guided and independent practice must be provided. If some students give one or two possibilities, they are beginning to understand and may need less direct instruction and practice. If most of the students indicate that there are an unlimited number of decimal numbers between 0.1 and 0.2, the teacher knows that for this unit, student understanding is nearly complete.

Heritage (2010) suggests that the information teachers derive from formative assessments, including questions, "is something they feed forward into their instruction to improve student learning" (p. 57). Quality questioning is an ideal way to determine if daily lessons are building on one another, moving students steadily forward in their learning and mastery of a given content area. If student responses to questions reveal that an overwhelming percentage of students are not ready for the lesson planned for the next day, as evidenced by incorrect or incomplete responses to formative questions, teachers have evidence that suggests the need to reteach. On the other hand, if student responses to such teacher questions reveal no learning gaps, the teacher is advised to accelerate the class's learning about the topic in question.

Formative assessment and feedback can help students understand their progress; equally as important, they can help teachers know how to proceed instructionally because in assessing what students understand and have learned, teachers learn how well they have taught and what they might do differently for better results. A common complaint among teachers is "I *taught* it; they just didn't *learn* it." A more accurate summary would be "If the students haven't *learned* it, then I haven't *taught* it."

The feedback to teachers—and its use by teachers—is in many respects more important to student learning than is feedback to students. When teachers become learners about their own teaching—when they reflect on,

> When as many as half the students in a class answer a clear question incorrectly or fail to meet a particular criterion, it is not a student learning problem—it is a teaching problem. Whatever strategy the teacher used, whatever examples were employed, or whatever explanation was offered, it simply did not work.
>
> –Guskey (2007, p. 20)

analyze the effectiveness of, and intentionally try different strategies—they make teaching visible and can make corrections and adaptations for improvement (Hattie, 2009, p. 173). That is, as teachers learn about the effectiveness of instructional strategies, not only can they effect change in their own teaching strategies but they can also suggest areas in which students require additional study or need to try different learning strategies.

CONNECTIONS: DEVELOPING LEARNER CAPACITY

Put simply, the only point of asking questions is to raise issues about which the teacher needs information or about which the student needs to think.

—Paul Black, Christine Harrison, Clare Lee,
Bethan Marshall, & Dylan Wiliam (2003, p. 42)

In this chapter, we have explored the dynamic relationship between quality questioning and formative assessment. By harnessing quality questioning for the purposes of formative assessment, teachers can also enhance metacognition, engagement, and self-efficacy among their students.

Student Metacognition

Remember this part of the vision for student learning presented in Chapter 1?

> *These students understand that meaningful learning is a process that occurs over time, and they routinely monitor their progress in a variety of ways. Among these are the processing of teacher formative feedback, the skillful use of preestablished criteria or rubrics to self-assess and self-monitor, and informal reflection on their progress toward understanding new concepts.*

This vision is grounded in cognitive science research, which provides important insights into thinking and learning. An important research summary from the National Research Council (2001) indicates that people who "monitor their own understanding" (p. 78) as they learn are better at retaining what they learn than those who do not self-monitor. According to the Council's summary, studies of metacognition have shown that people who continually monitor their own thinking and comprehension actually remember more.

Teachers can do many things to help students learn how to monitor and self-assess, and they can encourage students to do it regularly. Asking students to reflect on their learning, for instance, helps them learn how to think about *what* and *how* they have learned. Many of the strategies in Resource B ask students to reflect in this manner. Teachers can ensure that students not only write but also talk about their learning with at least one other student. Cooperative groups and partners provide opportunities for students to learn from others as they share their strategies for learning. Each of the following questions is related to formative assessment and to developing students' metacognition:

- **What am I seeking to learn or be able to do?** Formative assessment questions are most commonly posed by teachers; however, the cycle of student learning and thinking (Figure 1.2) suggests that students can learn to monitor their own progress toward learning goals. As responsible learners, they are able to ask and answer this question: *What am I seeking to learn or be able to do?* This ability is critical for formative assessment. After all, it is impossible for people to adequately assess progress toward a goal if they don't have a clear idea of what it is they are aiming for.
- **What do I currently know or think about the topic? Is it accurate?** Preassessments, a particular type of formative assessment, are integral parts of learning. To know where we are in relationship to the goal, we need to identify what we know. Know, want to know, and learned (KWL) or other such common strategies can help students answer this question.
- **How will I make personal meaning of this content?** For students to use formative feedback, they need to make meaning of the learning

goals by translating them into learning targets or "I can" statements. Otherwise, they are merely going through the motions of learning. Knowing that teachers expect them to self-assess heightens accountability. So does knowing that the purpose behind teachers' questions is to discover what they, the students, think—not to tell them what they *should* be thinking.

- **How am I monitoring my learning and progress?** As students begin to take responsibility for their own learning, they use reflection and self-assessment—and it helps if they have seen these behaviors modeled by teachers. As students begin to understand that they can indeed monitor their own learning, they better understand (1) the purpose of various learning activities, (2) what success looks like, (3) how close they are to achieving that success, and (4) what they might do to accomplish their goals.

- **To what extent am I developing response-ability?** As students become accountable to formulate responses to questions and to assess their own performance and use feedback, they develop personal responsibility as learners.

- **What have I learned? How can I take my learning to the next level?** Students who take responsibility for their learning outcomes generally understand and use self-monitoring to think about how to extend their learning. As these students work cooperatively with others in small and large groups, they ask and answer these questions through discussion and dialogue.

Student Engagement

We can identify no strategy with more potential to improve the relationship between students and teachers and between students and the content they are learning than formative assessment. Through the process of setting learning targets, students better understand the *what* and *why* of the unit under study. Classroom activities are no longer solely about *She told me to do it, so I'm going to do it.* Students who are actively engaged in formative assessment can answer the all-too-common question *Why do we have to learn this?*

As teachers use student responses to questions as data that can inform their teaching and provide students with feedback, all members of the classroom learning community understand the importance of clarity in establishing what is being learned and why, believe that only through assessment can they identify gaps in their learning, and view learning as a process. Members of a classroom in which formative feedback is used are continually thinking about ways to improve. Students and teachers alike are willing to identify and try new ways of teaching and learning.

In this classroom, students and teachers develop a relationship based on trust. The "teacher as judge" or "gotcha" mentality is not a part of this classroom culture. As teachers engage in formative assessment, they more often use strategies that engage all students (such as those described in

Resource B), rather than relying on the traditional Initiation-Response-Evaluation (IRE) pattern, in which one student responds to one teacher's question. Teachers can further engage students by helping them learn how to self-assess their own learning. "Providing students with an opportunity to reflect on their current performance and to set personal goals for improvement promotes their engagement in and ownership of the ongoing assessment process" (Ainsworth & Viegut, 2006, p. 60).

Student Self-Efficacy

Many low-achieving students play the game of school without any hope of winning. Their chances decrease each year. They sit in the back of the class and let the "smart kids" answer teacher questions. Often, they are not listening to teacher questions. They are not engaged nor do they seem to care about being engaged. Teachers call on them occasionally—and sometimes they are surprised by guessing correctly at the answer. It is a surprise to them when something is wrong as well as when something is right. When an answer is wrong, there's rarely a second chance. Many of these students have decided they cannot be successful. They don't know what they are supposed to be learning or why they should be learning it.

In most classrooms, teachers are in control of assessment, which is delivered in the form of a grade or a final judgment. Students who perform poorly assume it is their destiny; they rarely question how things could be different for them. The process of formative assessment changes this dynamic. As we reported earlier, formative assessment improves the learning of all students, but it appears to have more of a positive effect on low achievers than on mid- to high-achieving students (Black & Wiliam, 1998b).

When formative assessment is important in a classroom, students assume control of their own learning: They know what and why they are learning; they understand how learning will be assessed; and they increasingly learn how to reflect, monitor, and self-assess so that they have increasing ownership of the learning process. Students "learn to gather evidence about their own learning and to use that information to choose from a growing collection of strategies for success" (Moss & Brookhart, 2009, p. 10). Students come to understand that what they do is directly related to their success or lack of success in accomplishing learning targets. In many ways, this is the definition of efficacy: the belief that what I do determines my success or lack of success. Self-efficacy empowers students in ways that traditional learning structures and traditional schools do not. Quality questioning as formative assessment builds academic self-efficacy.

5

Developing Response-Ability

*In What Ways Can Teachers Cultivate
and Nourish Student Responsibility for Learning?*

FOCUS QUESTIONS

1. In what ways can teachers partner with students to encourage them to assume increased responsibility for their own learning?

2. What norms and strategies encourage students to think about questions and formulate responses to teacher questions?

3. How do collaborative learning and discussion promote student motivation and assumption of responsibility for learning?

4. Why is it important to encourage student questions? How do they relate to student engagement? To student responsibility?

The lesson sticks with you when you work collaboratively. I remember more when I work with my team members. Also, I am motivated to take the time to learn things on my own because I know I'll be asked to help someone else. But I also learn from my teammates; everyone has something to contribute.

—9th-grade female student, Winterboro High School, Alabama

In *The Global Achievement Gap*, Tony Wagner (2008) offers sobering facts that show American students at great disadvantage in comparison to students from other industrialized nations. He recommends "seven survival skills for teens today," including these four:

- Critical thinking and problem solving
- Collaboration
- Effective oral and written communications
- Curiosity

These may be considered the Four Cs—critical thinking, collaboration, communications, and curiosity—used by thoughtful teachers who understand the real-world challenges that face their students. Other authors and organizations have identified skills essential for surviving and thriving in this new world. In one form or another, the Four Cs are included in the recommendations of many—for example, the Partnership for 21st Century Skills, the Organization for Economic Co-operation and Development, and Howard Gardner.

Are these 21st-century skills yet another layer of skills and abilities that teachers are being asked to teach? This question, which can spark debate and even controversy, deserves serious consideration.

In one sense, the forenamed skills are not add-ons; rather, they constitute the basics for learning. Consider this: In 2011, as this book goes to press, we know more about how students learn than we have ever known; in 18 months or less, we are likely to know twice as much, thanks to the information explosion. One thing we know is that a prescription for failure to learn includes what is all too often found in American classrooms: students sitting passively as they do (or pretend to do) what the teacher tells them, with little or no understanding of why and working problems and completing assignments that have little or no relevance to their lives, in isolation from others, with little interaction or talking. This is the reality because very few teachers know and use current information about how students learn best. Twenty-first-century skills, when viewed from this perspective, are not add-ons but integral to teaching and learning.

On the other hand, these are skills that have not been explicitly taught in schools, although they have been advocated for years. What has changed is that they are now essential—no excuses—because they are required for navigating and functioning in modern times. As recently as the late 1970s, the discrete set of knowledge that teachers dispensed in schools had a reasonably long shelf life. The new reality is that much of today's knowledge will be outdated soon; consequently, we need to teach not only facts and concepts but also the skills with which to learn: thinking critically and analytically, asking questions, formulating hypotheses, and collaboratively discussing options.

Students of all ages need to know how to take responsibility for learning. That is, they need to know how to identify a problem, pose questions as they search for possible solutions, analyze sources for reliability and accuracy, and evaluate and select an approach to solve the problem—all the while working in teams. This is the world in which the modern workforce lives; this needs to be the work of today's students.

Throughout this book, we refer to the imagined dichotomy between teaching content and teaching thinking skills. Students learn content by learning and applying thinking skills successfully and responsibly; without the thinking part, students will not learn the content—or they will learn it just long enough to pass a test and forget it. Because we live in an information-rich world that cannot be fully known, our students need these skills not only to learn in school but, more important, in order to learn beyond school. "Developing lifelong learners," an aspiration embedded in many schools' mission statements, must now become the reality in every classroom.

Thinking Through QQ: What do you believe about the relationship between thinking and learning? In four or five sentences, articulate a rationale for focusing on student learning through thinking.

The Four Cs named at the beginning of this chapter are not all-inclusive, but they are a good starting point for thinking about what will give our students the ability to continue to learn throughout their lives. These skills are intrinsically linked to success in the workplace of the 21st century because they can be applied to tomorrow's problems, which have not yet been imagined. Successful workers are always thinking—of the implications of a plan or policy, of how to solve a potential problem—and they do this thinking with others. Their success hinges on their ability to network, communicate with colleagues and clients, and listen well to understand customer needs.

Critical thinking, collaboration, communication, and curiosity constitute essential skills needed for learning in school, for success in the workplace, and for contributing to and participating in our democratic form of government. This last role cannot be overlooked. Most of our students are or will be voters—democratic decision makers who, now more than ever, need to be able to synthesize and analyze information from multiple sources, work together for the common good, and ask probing questions about the many and complex issues that face our country and our world. Citizens need to be able to discuss these questions with others, demonstrating respect for diverse points of view and articulating their own positions clearly. As illustrated in the Venn diagram in Figure 5.1, the essential skills for all three areas of life—school, work, and citizenship—overlap.

Figure 5.1   Relationship of Skills for Learning and Living

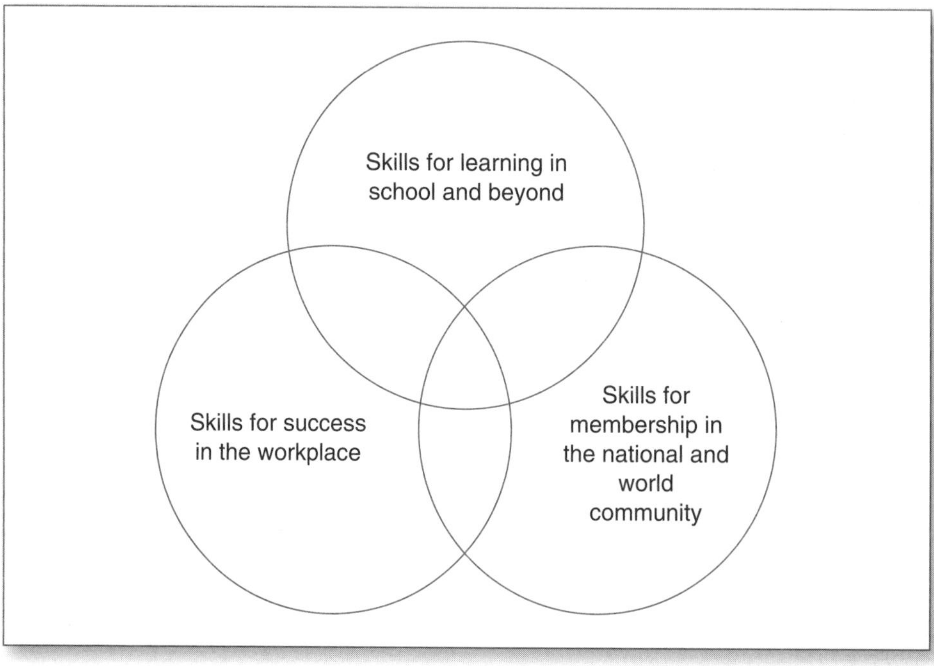

This discussion brings us to an issue that permeates the entire Framework for Thinking Through Quality Questioning: How do students develop response-ability for their own learning? What kinds of structures and processes encourage them to step up to the plate instead of waiting to be spoon-fed?

In the years since we wrote our first book on quality questioning, we find ourselves taking a broader view of student participation. It is not just about being engaged equitably by answering a fair share of questions, although that is important. It is also about being response-able in the larger sense of the word. Developing student response-ability helps build student capacity to articulate a position clearly and to listen to others' views, assess them, and learn from them. It has to do with students being involved in the process of learning and accepting responsibility to (1) pay attention to and interpret a question from a teacher or another student;

(2) think about what they know about the topic in question and occasionally form their own questions about the topic; (3) communicate their thoughts to others in a clear manner, extending their ideas when given the opportunity or when prompted to explain; and (4) be open to hearing other points of view about the question—knowing that they will learn more by hearing others' ideas on a given topic. Response-ability is taking ownership of learning; being proactive, not reactive; seeking to actively learn, not passively receive information; and collaborating with one's peers to both investigate and create questions. Throughout this chapter, we use **response-ability** (as opposed to *responsibility*) in the context of planned and deliberate development of these skills and habits of mind.

Thinking Through QQ: Do you agree that the Four Cs contribute to response-ability—both for learning in school and for lifelong learning? If you do, in what ways do you believe each of the Four Cs contributes to response-ability? If not, what is your basis for disagreement?

The elements of student thinking, introduced in Chapter 1 as the Cycle of Student Thinking and Learning (Figure 1.2), cannot occur without students taking responsibility for their own learning. In this chapter, we will consider four ways to help develop student response-ability:

- Hold students accountable
- Develop student capacity to ask quality questions
- Provide opportunities for students to learn collaboratively
- Teach skills of collaborative discussion

HOLD STUDENTS ACCOUNTABLE

In our previous book, *Quality Questioning: Research-Based Practice to Engage Every Learner* (Walsh & Sattes, 2005), we discussed at length why and how to *engage all students* in responding. We advocated that teachers intentionally use alternate response formats to provide equal opportunities for students to respond (and, subsequently, to learn). We recommended the use of a variety of strategies for answering (as opposed to calling on one student at a time) to change the traditional pattern of highly competent students benefiting disproportionately from teachers calling on them frequently. These "target" students, as they are referred to in the literature, speak three to four times more frequently than do nontarget students (Jones, 1990; Sadker & Sadker, 1985).

The use of alternate response formats begins to change the paradigm of traditional classrooms, in which one student answers each question. Students are more fully engaged in these classrooms. However, the teacher is still in control. Teachers who use these kinds of strategies find that more students participate and more seem interested during classroom interactions. This does not automatically translate to students taking responsibility for their own thinking and learning. Teachers must be intentional in giving ownership of learning to students.

Give Students a Reason to Participate

As many as 30% of high school students drop out of school every year. Many have passing grades, which demonstrates that they have the ability to continue; it has been said that these students have the *skill* but not the *will* to stay in school and graduate. In other words, boredom is the primary reason for failure to graduate (Wagner, 2008, p. xxv). In today's classrooms, despite all the research and literature about the importance of student engagement in relevant content with appropriate rigor and meaningful relationships, researchers find that elementary students spend more than 90% of classroom time in their seats listening to the teacher (Wagner, p. 68). During this teacher talk-time, questions are undoubtedly posed. But, as we have mentioned, many teachers call on only one student to answer each question. Frequently, these are volunteers, who eagerly raise or wave their arms in the air, look the teacher in the eye, and give other cues that they are ready and willing to answer.

The Initiation-Response-Evaluation (IRE) pattern often seen in classrooms can be likened to a baseball game wherein the teacher pitches every question, evaluates the answers (as umpire), catches the missed balls, and fields student answers by playing all other positions: first, second, and third base; outfield; and shortstop. What are students doing during this game? They are sitting passively, waiting for a turn at bat. They enter the batter's box one at a time, take a swing (sometimes successfully and sometimes not), and then return to the bench, where they wait to be called on—one at a time—to step up to the plate again. And they get only one strike, not three, so they seldom spend more than a few seconds at bat. No wonder students are bored! And, as we like to say, no wonder teachers are tired at the end of the day!

So how can teachers break this pattern? What is a winning game plan for keeping students engaged in thinking about and answering questions? The Framework for Thinking Through Quality Questioning suggests that teachers can coach their students to greater success by incorporating into their practice the interrelated components of quality questioning, as outlined in this book:

- Questions need to be interesting to students; the content must relate to the students' interests, prior knowledge, and experiences (Chapter 2).
- At least some of the questions must be thought provoking, that is, above the remember and understand levels of the Revised Bloom Taxonomy (Anderson & Krathwohl, 2001) and have more than one correct answer (Chapter 2).

- Questions must be deserving of thought and bookended on both sides of the response by time to think about answers (Chapter 3).
- Students understand that their answers may be challenged by other students or by the teacher; they know that just any answer is not sufficient, but rather they must be ready to provide examples or explain their thinking as to how they arrived at their answer (Chapter 3).
- Students learn how to reflect and to pose questions that help them assess where they are in relation to learning targets (Chapter 4).
- Classroom expectations must clearly communicate that all students will formulate answers to every question that is posed (Chapter 5).
- Respect for student ideas must be a norm in the classroom; both the teacher and the students listen and ask questions to fully understand others' responses (Chapters 2, 3, 4, 5, and 6).

Use Structures That Allow Students to Safely Formulate and Test Responses

In nearly every group we work with, a teacher comments, *I have a student who will not talk in class. I don't like to force her to speak when it makes her so uncomfortable. What can I do?* Many teachers face this challenge: the shy or insecure student who goes to extreme lengths to discourage the teacher from calling on her. Some avoid calling on such students because they fear it is too threatening. But what of our responsibility to develop that student's capacity to communicate? Don't we owe it to all of our students to help them learn to express their ideas and thoughts clearly and publicly?

Sometimes, teachers can help reticent students talk about their ideas by providing opportunities for them to respond to questions in pairs, where they can voice their ideas to just one other student. One structure is Think-Pair-Share, in which the teacher poses a question and allows time for each student to (a) formulate his responses, (b) talk to a partner about his answer, and then (c) share with the large group. For many students, talking to one person is less threatening than speaking to the entire class. Say Something, a tool for reading comprehension, also puts each student with a partner. The class is directed to read a short passage and then "say something" to their partner and listen as their partner says something to them about what they just read. Insight and Question (IQ) Pairs, another reading comprehension strategy, asks students to identify an insight and a question they have after reading a passage and to share and discuss with a partner. A more complex structure, Interview Design, provides the opportunity for students to pose a prepared question to other students, interviewing four or five students (one at a time), and then meeting with others in the group who posed the same question to summarize and discuss responses to the question. All of these structures have in common the provision of a nonthreatening environment in which a learner speaks to just one other person to respond to a question.

Thinking Through QQ: What are the benefits of using structures in which every student is engaged in responding to questions by talking to at least one other student?

These structures (described in Resource A) give students the opportunity to think and talk. Talking activates thinking; as students exchange ideas, usually the energy in the room increases because the students are more fully present and engaged. This came home to us recently as we saw a third-grade teacher ask, *What is a critic? Like a movie critic? A food critic?* Only one or two students raised their hands to answer; she called on one and then she said, *Talk about this question in your groups: What is a critic?* As students talked, they visibly became more engaged in thinking; they exchanged ideas; they were excited to figure it out; collectively, they arrived at an answer. It took only a couple of minutes to go from having only two students who were able or willing to answer to having everyone in the class ready to answer. At that point, all class members were prepared to listen to a student respond to the teacher's question and to gauge the correctness or incorrectness of their own answers.

Some teachers don't like to take the time to use collaborative response strategies, but it is important to give students time to think through their ideas and to connect new learning to what they already know. Because learning is a social activity, it can be said that as students talk, they are learning more about a given topic. The adage "the one who does the talking does the learning" is worth paying attention to. In many classrooms, *teachers* are doing the preponderance of the learning! Using collaborative response strategies or similar structures gives students an opportunity to process the information that is being shared, talk about what it means, and hear other students construct their own personal meaning by thinking aloud. At the same time, students are developing the Four Cs: critical thinking, collaboration, communication, and curiosity.

For teachers interested in assessing student understanding, the response structures mentioned earlier offer several advantages. First, they allow every student to give an answer. By randomly selecting learners to speak to the large group, teachers can hear samples of what pairs discussed and get a good fix on whether they should move on, clarify misconceptions, or provide further instruction on a topic. Certainly, when contrasted with hearing one student speak at a time, these structures are time-efficient because every student is responding to every question. It's true that teachers do not hear every student's answer, but neither do they hear an answer from every student when they call on one student at a time to speak.

This is not to say that there is no place in schooling for teacher talk; teacher presentations are frequently the best method for structuring content.

Jackie's son, for instance, teaches in a large university and sometimes has as many as 200 students in an introductory economics class. In that setting, presentations are, by necessity, the norm. However, he has adopted the practice of stopping every 15 to 20 minutes to pose a question that students figure out with a partner, applying the information that was just presented. Like his mother, he is a natural teacher; he finds that this strategy helps students stay engaged and interested. More important, it builds students' capacity to be response-able by giving them opportunities to make meaning of new content.

DEVELOP STUDENTS' CAPACITY TO ASK QUALITY QUESTIONS

Curiosity does not kill the cat—not in a classroom where teachers believe it is their job to develop students as questioners. In our last book, we encouraged teachers to help students learn how to ask good questions because it is a sign of student engagement and thinking. Our focus at the time was primarily on content-related student learning outcomes. We still believe that is important. But we also know that the ability to ask questions is increasingly important for life in our complex, rapidly changing world. Consider this: As Wagner (2008) interviewed CEOs about what they looked for in employees, the "ability to ask questions" appeared as a recurring theme. Wagner went so far as to state, "Problem-posing is more important than problem-solving" (p. 214).

Curiosity is one of the important skills of today's world; when teachers understand this, they value students who wonder, speculate, hypothesize, and imagine. When students ask true questions, from a position of not knowing but wanting to know, they are thinking deeply about a topic. Asking questions has been said to be an indication of a high level of engagement; students ask questions when they are interested and want to learn more than the teacher has suggested or offered.

Broadly speaking, there are three levels of student engagement (see Figure 5.2). The lowest level is complying. At this level, students are doing what the teacher has asked or directed. This is how "engagement" is defined on some classroom walk-throughs—as students engaging in the work that has been assigned to them by the teacher. Indeed, it is the first step to engagement—and it ranks far above napping, texting, or reading an unrelated book—but it does not demonstrate student responsibility for learning.

The middle level is committing. At this level, students are interested in the topic and mental lightbulbs may be coming on as students have realizations or insights about the content under study. They see connections between the content and their own lives; they see relevance. At this level, students can tell you what they are trying to learn and why—in their own words, not merely in the words of the teacher. They may find ways of adding to the learning experience by suggesting an activity or a resource that would help the group better understand.

Figure 5.2 Taxonomy of Student Engagement

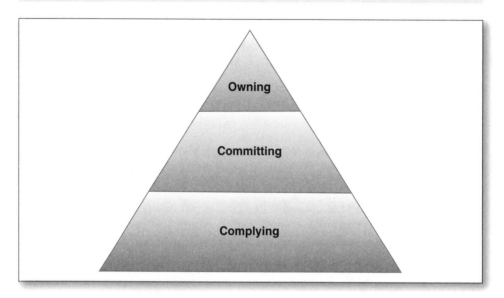

The highest level of student engagement is owning. At this level, students want to talk about the subject. As they leave class, they don't leave the content behind. They may bring up the topic with friends, in another class, or at the dinner table. They may use an Internet search engine, join a wiki or a blog, and begin pursuing it on their own. Students at this level of engagement make the learning their own. This top level of engagement is where we witness students posing questions to take them deeper in learning about the subject.

So how does a teacher help students develop the capacity to ask? They do this, in part, by making time for questions in class, by helping students understand the connection between questioning and learning, by modeling true questioning, and by explicitly teaching quality questioning skills to students.

Thinking Through QQ: What is your reaction to the Taxonomy of Student Engagement? At what level would you place the majority of students in your class(es) or school? What percentage of students in your class(es) or school would you place at the highest level of engagement?

Make Time for Questions

Do you remember, from Chapter 3, Mary Budd Rowe's (1986) puzzlement over how rarely she heard students pose questions in science classes? She found some classrooms that seemed to be exceptions, and when she explored how these classrooms differed from the majority, she discovered that they were distinguished by moments of teacher silence. It appears that, in terms of helping students think about the questions that are asked in class, silence is indeed golden.

In addition to allowing time for student answers, moments of silence can allow time for student questions. Student questions have not traditionally been on the radar screen for most educators. J. T. Dillon (1988) refers to traditional classroom questioning episodes as times in which students see their role as "answerers" of questions; indeed, in some classrooms, students speak only in answers. In these same classrooms, teachers own the role of "questioner." It is difficult, indeed brave, for students to break with tradition and, instead of answering, request permission to pose a question. Dillon argues that in many classrooms students don't have time to think long enough to formulate a question, given the barrage of questions directed at them by teachers. Hence the value of wait time: Not only do teachers, responders, and other students have time to think about a given response; they also have time to formulate a question: *Do I agree? Why is that the answer? Why isn't the answer this? What happened to cause that?*

> One of the simplest ways to permit student questions is to stop asking questions yourself.
>
> —J. T. Dillon (1983, p. 37)

One outcome of using wait times, especially Wait Time 2, is more student questions. As teachers help students understand the purpose and value of pauses, they can encourage student questions to emerge by affirming that the asking of questions by students is desired and, in fact, expected.

Understand the Value of Questions

Ask students why they don't ask questions in school, and some common themes will appear. A closer look at student comments on the matter (see Figure 5.3) suggests that a set of unspoken (and probably unintentional and unexamined) classroom norms are likely contributing to students' hesitancy to pose their own questions.

And yet there is the story (reported by Barell, 2003) of Nobel Prize-winning physicist Isadore Rabi, who claims his mother asked him every day after school not *What did you learn today?* but rather, *What good question did you ask today?* That mother knew the power of asking questions! She knew the importance of her son connecting with the material enough to be able to formulate a question in order to learn more.

 Norm: Be open to wondering and asking, not just to knowing and answering.

It might come as a surprise to many students that they are learning more when they are thinking about questions to ask related to the project or

Figure 5.3 Why Students Don't Ask Questions in School

Student Comment	Implicit Classroom Value or Norm
The teacher doesn't like questions.	Student questions are not important; we don't have time; they take us off-task; it's important to cover the content in the state standards.
Who cares about that stuff?	The content is not relevant or interesting; students are bored.
It's not cool.	Learning and achievement are not really valued by most students in this classroom. Students who appear to be too interested in school and learning are probably not successful socially.
I don't want to look dumb.	Students who ask questions must not have understood; asking questions shows you are not very smart.
That's not my job; that's the teacher's job.	The role of the teacher is to ask questions for which he already knows the answers. The role of the student is to give teachers the answers they already know. That's what they want to hear.

content under study than when they are answering teacher questions. Questioning is a natural way of learning: Something puzzles you, you begin to wonder about it, you formulate a question, and then you begin to try to answer it. When you want to know something, the motivation to learn is present; there's no stopping you! The literature about reading comprehension confirms the value of student-generated questions. Good readers ask themselves questions as they read (Rosenshine, Meister, & Chapman, 1996), and asking questions is related to improved reading comprehension.

The ability to ask good questions has become especially important in recent years because of the information explosion and the need for individuals to effectively manage their interactions with this information, both personally and professionally. People in all professions need to update their knowledge and skills continually through asking questions and seeking answers.

Thinking Through QQ: What is your view of the value of student questions and questioning? What would be the value of you and your colleagues engaging in dialogue about the need to focus on this skill?

For the many citizens who value active participation in the democratic functioning of their country, questions play an increasingly important role. Despite (and sometimes because of) the wealth of information that is widely available, questions related to today's social, political, and economic issues are more complex and more difficult to answer than ever. Consider a few of the issues around which voters need to make informed decisions:

- What is the best approach to dealing with the Israeli-Palestinian conflict? How did it begin? Whose problem is it?
- How can we ensure that all of our citizens receive affordable, quality health care? Is that a responsibility of the government or is that the personal responsibility of each citizen? What can we do to curb the soaring costs of health care?
- What constitutes an extremist Muslim? What is the basis of extremists' hatred for the Western world? What can we do to try to establish more peaceful relations in the Eastern world? What are the biggest barriers to peaceful coexistence? What are the factors working in favor of peace?
- Why is crime so high in the United States compared with other industrialized countries?
- How is immigration today different from immigration at the turn of the 20th century? What data are available about the numbers of immigrants over the past 100 years? How is immigration policy (legality and illegality) established?

These are complex issues that citizens need to read and think about, and such research takes patience. Yet the digital natives in our classrooms are accustomed to quick and often ready-made answers (think of how often you've heard them say, *I Googled for the answer*). The average website visit is two seconds (Sprenger, 2009, p. 34); that is hardly long enough for complex thinking! How can we help our students learn to question information so that they know whether it is valid and reliable?

> Problem-posing education . . . is a most natural way for students to become involved in their own learning. We begin to think when we recognize a problematic situation, and from this follows a process of inquiry.
>
> —Barell (1995, p. 91)

Model True Questioning

Often the questions that we teachers ask in class are not true questions because we already know the answers—and students know that we know. So they may consider a question-and-answer session as a test rather than an exploration.

If we want students to learn to ask questions, we need to model wondering and true questioning. We need to ask questions for which we may not know the answers, for which we are considering different possibilities, for which we are interested in what students think. When we read aloud to the class, we can stop and ask ourselves a question: *I wonder what Ellen was thinking when she heard that noise?* Then we can engage in answering it aloud so that students can hear our thinking process. Or while reading a social studies article, we might ask, *I know the Berlin Wall was torn down in 1989. I wonder if it was a spontaneous occurrence as people got excited and began to tear apart the wall or if it happened after some official announcement as a planned event?*

As students experience their teachers asking questions, they will begin to learn what questioning looks and sounds like. Hopefully, they will begin to ask true questions to peers, to teachers, and to family members.

Explicitly Teach Questioning Skills

To help students learn questioning, it helps to teach them processes or structures that can be used repeatedly in the classroom. One such process is the well-known Know, Want to Know, Learned (KWL), in which the teacher asks students to answer the following three questions (individually, in small groups, or in a large group):

1. What do you think you know about this topic? (K)

2. What do you want to learn about this topic? (W)

3. What have you learned about this topic? (L)

Asking "What do you *think* you know?" rather than "What do you know?" causes students to question themselves, to be reflective, and to consider that there might actually be a difference between what they know and *think* they know. This realization can spark curiosity, and students will generate questions to identify what they want to know more about; as students identify the focus of their own learning, they correspondingly experience an increase in motivation and ownership (Barell, 2003, p. 105). This builds the capacity of student response-ability.

Barell (2003) and others advocate inquiry-based learning or problem-based learning (PBL), in which students are challenged to pose questions and work to find answers. When students are engaged in PBL, they tend to own the learning (see Figure 5.2) as they pose questions; they make choices that increase their motivation to learn; and teachers share the control of the learning with the students. PBL requires higher-level thinking and gives students experience in developing the life skill of identifying, solving, and reporting on a problem. We suggest that teachers use a structure such as Know, Question, Strategy (KQS × 3) (depicted in Figure 5.4) as an organizer when conducting a PBL experience with students.

A structure that explicitly teaches questioning skills is Question, Question, which works well with collaborative groups or pairs of students. As you explore a topic, stop and ask students to think about what they find interesting about the topic and would like to discuss further. Ask them, in pairs, to formulate questions for discussion. Help them identify the qualities of good discussion questions: open-ended, with more than one correct answer; interesting to students; relevant to their

Figure 5.4 KQS × 3—Organizer for Student Planning, Investigating, and Assessing Inquiry-Based Learning

Knowledge	Question	Strategy
Planning		
What do we think we know about this subject?	What questions will drive our inquiry?	What strategies will we use to investigate and learn more about this topic?
Investigating		
How are we extending and deepening our knowledge?	What additional questions are emerging?	What other strategies and resources do we need?
Assessing		
What new knowledge and understandings have we acquired?	What lingering questions do we have?	How can we strategically apply our new knowledge in other settings?

lives; and helpful in presenting a different perspective and encouraging deeper exploration. As students are learning this strategy, you may want to suggest stems that would help them formulate their discussion questions, such as the following:

- I wonder about . . .
- How are these alike and different?
- What would you predict might happen if . . .
- What are the key elements of . . .

- What are the implications of . . .
- What might the consequences be if . . .

After the class discusses one of these questions, you might use the opportunity to help students learn more about quality questions. Reflect aloud on how the discussion question served to interest students and how it might have been phrased differently to work better at prompting deeper thinking. You might use or modify the rubric presented in Chapter 2 to help students self-assess or use a critical friend to assess their questions.

Thinking Through QQ: What strategies have you used to encourage student questioning? What strategies might you consider using in the future?

Learn to Question Media Sources as to Reliability and Accuracy

Give a student a question to answer and she will learn the passage she has just read. Teach her how to ask questions and she will learn how to learn for the rest of her life.

—Gavelek &
Raphael (1985, p. 103)

As students and teachers turn to the Internet for answers with ever-increasing frequency, it is incumbent upon us to learn (and help students learn) how to evaluate the information that we hear (on radio, television, YouTube, etc.) and read (whether on the Internet, in e-mail messages, or in print). Barell (2003) cites John McPeck, who partially defines critical thinking as "a certain skepticism, or suspension of assent, towards a given statement, established norm or mode of doing things" (p. 119). This seems to be a healthy approach in a world overrun with information—much of it of uncertain veracity.

A quick look at the Internet (yes, we do it too!) revealed over 6 million results for the search "evaluating information on the Internet." Many university library websites appeared to be worthwhile. We suggest working with students, depending on their developmental level, to cocreate criteria by which to evaluate the accuracy and reliability of information. Consider the categories described here—author, bias, currency, and details, or A-B-C-D—as a starting point for your work with students:

Author   Who wrote the piece? Is authorship acknowledged? If so, can you find credible references to this author? Who published it? Is there a known company's logo on the material? Does it appear to have been refereed? Is the publisher/source credible in the discipline to which the content of the article is directed?

Bias   What is the point of view? Does the author acknowledge her biases? What is the slant or spin of the author?

Currency: What is the date of the writing? Has it been updated recently? Does it appear to be a part of an ongoing project, which has as its mission to keep current on the topic?

Details: Is the information verifiable? Does the author cite reliable sources? Can you find other sources to validate the accuracy of the information? Does the author present data to support his claims? Does the evidence appear to be objective and reliable?

PROVIDE OPPORTUNITIES FOR STUDENTS TO LEARN COLLABORATIVELY

"**Cooperative learning** is the instructional use of small groups so that students work together to maximize their own and each other's learning" (Johnson & Johnson, 1999, p. 5). It is one of the most frequently studied instructional strategies in the education literature, with findings that yield consistent results: Structuring learning opportunities in groups can result in significant learning benefits for students. Increases in learning outcomes are reported to be higher for low-income students and minority students. And there are advantages accruing to students beyond improved learning outcomes. Studies have documented improved student self-concept, time on task, and social interaction skills (Darling-Hammond et al., 2008; Marzano, Pickering, & Pollock, 2001).

Cooperative learning is *not* merely seating students in groups and giving them individual work to perform side-by-side. If students are passively working on teacher-generated assignments with another person or persons, they are not learning cooperatively. Cooperative learning requires interdependence among learners: It involves students talking together; figuring things out together; making decisions, planning, and solving problems collaboratively; and assuming responsibility for their own and others' learning.

For teachers who don't currently teach through cooperative instruction, it can be difficult to transition to this way of teaching. Students throughout the United States "almost never work in teams" (Wagner, 2008, p. 68). Indeed, most students spend a majority of time in school completing seatwork or passively listening to teachers present information (Rotherham & Willingham, 2009, p. 20). Teachers find it hard to give up control and to trust that students will adequately assume responsibility for their learning. Wagner asserts, "The 'Old World of School' is still run more by command and control than are many companies . . . and students are accustomed to having teachers tell them what to do" (p. 26). This desire for control creates a conundrum: Teachers don't want to give up control, but they complain that "students aren't responsible" or that "students want to be spoon-fed." This cycle can be broken only by intention and effort. Those of us who maintain control of learning are not allowing students to assume response-ability; for students to take it on, we must give it up. Collaborative learning is a strategy that allows teachers to provide structure while appropriately handing off to students increased response-ability for decision making and control of learning.

Help Groups Establish Ground Rules and Regularly Reflect on Their Use

Beth was in a classroom recently where, as the class was transitioning from small-group work to whole-class structuring of information, the teacher asked, *How are we doing in our group work? Is there anything we need to discuss?* One student said the groups were *great*. The teacher probed to get more descriptive information about the work of the groups. A different student elaborated by commenting that everyone was contributing. The teacher asked a follow-up question: *What is your evidence for that statement? Do you have a system for keeping track of participation?* The student could not demonstrate that everyone was involved and participating, but he believed that it was happening. The teacher asked, *How might you check on that? What kind of data might you collect to see if everyone is participating equitably?* The groups took time to consider the question; each group came up with a strategy for monitoring participation. The teacher gave them feedback: *I'm glad that we're talking about this. I've noticed that some people are talking a lot more than others, and I want us to remember our ground rules that enable productive group work.*

 Norm: Monitor your talk so others can contribute.

POTENTIAL GROUND RULES FOR COLLABORATIVE GROUPS

- Be open to and respect all points of view.
- Listen with an open mind and expect to learn from one another.
- Accept responsibility for active and equitable participation by each group member.
- Check for understanding: Before you counter an idea, be sure you fully understand what has been said.
- Allow think time—before and after a group member speaks.
- Welcome questions.

None of us comes to school knowing how to work in teams effectively. These are learned skills. The establishment of rules for group work—and time to reflect on how we are doing as a team—is one way to scaffold the development of collaboration skills. A set of procedures might be established by each small group or by the entire classroom for all groups.

Clearly defined roles are another aid to helping groups function well. Typical roles in a cooperative group activity include facilitator, timekeeper, reporter, recorder, and materials manager. Depending on the task, additional roles may be required. Teachers can facilitate group work by suggesting and defining roles that are helpful to a given task, monitoring to see that roles are rotated among group members, and occasionally stopping for small- and large-group reflection on how well the roles are working for them.

Provide Structures to Increase Collaborative Skills

Teachers can introduce students to structures that help groups be productive in learning situations. Protocols such as Final Word, Save the Last Word for Me, Questioning Circle, the Four A's, and other text-based strategies (see Resource A) can enable a group to process and share information, providing structure to facilitate contributions from all students. Jigsaw, a cooperative learning strategy in which each member of the home group becomes expert on a different topic in order to share with and teach others in their home group, is another way to organize groups for productive work. For groups engaged in overtime projects such as inquiry-based learning or PBL, such protocols can assist group members in identifying problems, posing questions, planning strategies for study, and preparing reports to share with interested parties.

In Chapter 2, we spotlighted Winterboro High School, a school that transformed itself through PBL. Two salient features of PBL are the questions that

---

Student Comments About the Value of Collaboration

It is easier to learn and also to retain information when you complete work with other people. Collaboration is working together to achieve a set goal that you can't accomplish on your own. Oftentimes, you need others to complete a project. I am better when I work in a group because I'm learning to be responsible for keeping others on track.

—12th-grade male student

I prefer not having to do an entire project by myself. I like it when others have my back. And if someone in your group doesn't understand, you can help them rather than waiting for the teacher. When you help out a classmate, you remember better because you have taught them. You have people who look to you for answers. When you're not in a group, everyone depends on the teacher for answers rather than asking classmates for help. One of the major benefits I see from PBL is that we're learning to work with others—and we won't be working alone when we enter the workforce.

—12th-grade female student

focus and drive student investigations and the collaborative learning structures that engage teams of students in this inquiry-based learning. Jennifer Barnett, the teacher leader who facilitates much of the PBL design work at the high school, interviewed a number of Winterboro students regarding their perception of the collaborative nature of their learning. Their comments are featured in the sidebar (page 123) titled "Student Comments About the Value of Collaboration." Jennifer interviewed these students in a small focus group and reported, *Even when answering these questions, the group said it was better to answer as a team rather than individually because you are able to elaborate on each other's ideas, which provides better responses.*

Some strategies build on the creative thinking that is more evident when we collaborate than when we work alone. Some structures that promote out-of-the-box thinking include Table Rounds (groups discuss issues and record notes and pictures on paper tablecloths), Ink Think (a structure for nonverbal mind-map creation in which members of a group learn to "listen" to one another's written ideas), Affinity Mapping (helps groups analyze and organize ideas into categories), and Synectics that employ analogies and metaphors to extend thinking.

Thinking Through QQ: Reflect on your current use of collaborative structures. How do you prepare students for work in teams? What protocols have you used with what success? Which of the protocols mentioned in the previous paragraphs might be appropriate for your classroom?

TEACH SKILLS OF COLLABORATIVE DISCUSSION

J. T. Dillon (1988), one of our primary sources as we began the study of questioning, learning, and thinking some 20 years ago, makes a helpful distinction between two main contexts for questioning in schools: (1) recitation, which follows the traditional IRE format, in which students answer questions that have one correct answer, speak only to the teacher, and receive evaluations of their answers, and (2) discussion, which is initiated by the posing of an open-ended question that is subject to answers from multiple points of view, in which students speak to one another (not just to the teacher) and both answer and pose questions. Our work with teachers has helped us understand the importance of students' understanding the difference between these two contexts and teachers' establishing rules or procedures to follow in each context.

Discussion allows us to hear different points of view; to speak aloud to clarify our own thinking; and to understand that in this complex world, many questions have no single, correct answer. The most powerful learning in groups comes from skillful, collaborative discussions. Unfortunately, students, and most adults, do not have the skills to engage in what we are terming collaborative discussions. Most students don't develop the skills in school because they have little opportunity. "Unfortunately, according to Kamil and colleagues (2008), this kind of discussion currently accounts for an average of only 1.7 minutes per 60 minutes of classroom instruction" (Kamil cited in Lemke & Coughlin, 2008, p. 56).

Clearly, one of the problems is that we don't spend much time discussing in schools. But a greater part of the problem is that students rarely, if ever, see discussion modeled skillfully—inside or outside of school. Much of what passes for discussion today involves little listening to or understanding of others' points of view. Discussion has been likened to a ping-pong game where comments fly back and forth, with little time to process or understand: We tend to listen with our own ideas in mind—not to fully understand what the other person is saying or means to say. Participants frequently make judgments of one another's comments rather than probe for deeper understanding. When someone says something with which we agree, we are quick to second the idea. When someone says something with which we don't agree, we either argue for our opinion or keep quiet (not giving voice to our beliefs). The outcome is that some win and others lose—and sometimes, no one wins.

In regular (undisciplined) discussions of the nature we described, there is very little reflection time or silence. As a result, participants tend to be reactive; they get defensive and argumentative. Rarely do they stop to explore the cause of their differences; rather, they make assumptions and continue without checking them for accuracy. Few of us, in a heated discussion, are deterred from our beliefs by facts or evidence; rarely are we asked to present the criteria against which we make judgments.

So what do we mean when we advocate for collaborative discussion? Thinkers such as Howard Gardner make a compelling case that we need to learn to listen and understand other points of view. In his book *Five Minds for the Future*, Gardner (2006) asserts that a "respectful mind" is essential for operating in a global community: "In a world where all are interlinked, intolerance or disrespect is no longer a viable option" (p. 5). By doing real, meaningful work in teams, students can develop tolerance as they learn and use effective skills for communication. They learn, as Gardner asserts, that "a perspective may be different without being defective" (p. 114). This is counter to current American culture, which is increasingly characterized by polarized views about governmental leaders, social issues, and personal relationships.

In *Controversy in the Classroom: The Democratic Power of Discussion*, Diana Hess (2009) argues that the teaching of discussion skills is essential preparation for living in a democratic society. She believes that schools are the places where this happens best, and although her background is social studies, she sees increasing utility for the discussion of controversial issues in science, math, health, psychology, and literature classes. Through her research, she has learned that teachers who use discussion skillfully in the classroom "teach intentionally *for* and *with* discussion" (p. 55). They teach *for discussion*, meaning their goal is to help students learn how to engage in discussion about authentic problems in today's world so they can make educated decisions as members of our democracy. They also teach *with discussion*, that is, discussion is a pedagogical tool with which they teach content, critical thinking, and communication skills.

Prepare Students

In order to be successful in using discussion as a learning or teaching strategy, teachers need to ensure that students are prepared to participate—that they know the content under discussion as well as the process of collaborative discussion. Sometimes discussions can be profitable as an introduction to a unit or lesson, and teachers can use it as formative assessment: an opportunity to assess student knowledge and understanding and to identify misconceptions. In this use of discussion, students will not have very much preparation with regard to content. More often, teachers use discussion as a culminating activity, in which students actively use what they have learned about a topic in order to integrate and apply their knowledge.

It is not an effective use of discussion to bring up a subject just for the purpose of discussion without preparing students for productive talk or planning a follow-up to the discussion. This type of "discussion" has helped earn the practice a bad name among teachers, as such discussions often turn into occasions for sharing ignorance or teachers' promotions of their own points of view—neither of which happens in collaborative discussion.

To prepare students for the process of discussion, it is helpful to talk with them about the purposes of discussion, as distinct from more typical classroom questioning. Discussion helps develop all of the Four Cs introduced at the beginning of the chapter: Students practice critical thinking as they think aloud to clarify their thinking. Not anything goes. In skillful discussion, students are expected to provide evidence for their statements, opinions, and judgments. They take their learning deeper as they apply what they've learned to new contexts. Discussion also helps in the development and application of communication skills such as improved listening skills and the ability to express thoughts clearly. Discussion is an essential skill of collaboration; students hear many points of view and, with respect for diverse viewpoints, learn from their peers. At its best, discussion encourages curiosity. Students want to know more about others' ideas; might they be more correct than their own? They speculate, hypothesize, and question.

 Norm: Listen with respect to other points of view in order to fully understand and learn.

Scaffold Discussion Skills With Ground Rules and Sample Probes for Clarification

Students need to learn how to distinguish between regular discussions and collaborative, skillful discussions. Establish ground rules, with student input, to move the discussion to a more skillful level. Here are some sample ground rules that teachers sometimes use:

- Speak to one another, not only to the teacher.
- Don't interrupt when another is speaking; signal the teacher to put your name on a "speaker's list" so that everyone who wants to speak gets an opportunity.
- Before you speak, summarize what the person who spoke prior to you said; check to make sure you understood correctly.
- Listen, listen, and listen. If you don't understand another's comment or point of view, ask a question to clarify.
- Withhold judgments; keep an open mind by asking, "What can I learn from this person?"
- Defend your points; provide evidence that is reliable and valid.
- If you haven't heard from someone in the group, ask that person what he thinks.

As students listen to understand others—not to push their own points of view—they refrain from judgment. They ask questions to clarify their own understanding, not to force others to defend their points of view. The most unproductive result of undisciplined thinking is that we make judgments about what people say before we fully understand what they are saying. As we make a judgment to agree or disagree, we stop listening to understand and begin thinking about what *we* think about the issue. When that happens, the opportunity to learn from one another ceases.

To help students stay engaged in the collaborative discussion, give them ideas about how to ask for clarification when peers make statements that are not clear. Suggest they follow up with questions or statements such as these:

- Can you give an example?
- I'd like to hear more of your thinking.
- Please say more.
- What do you mean when you say . . . ?

Scaffold Discussion Skills With Processes

Teachers can use interactive processes to help students prepare to discuss in the large group or in their smaller collaborative groups. Simply displaying the written question and asking students to take time to reflect in writing about their views can help students become prepared to engage.

Asking students to talk with a partner (Think-Pair-Share) before discussing with the larger group helps students think through their ideas verbally. A process called Peoplegraph asks students to decide "where they stand" with regard to agreeing or disagreeing with a statement and then to discuss the reasons for their stance with others nearby who have taken a similar position. Hearing and sharing ideas about the issue in small groups such as this helps build student confidence and prepares them for large-group discussion.

Another process that helps students be intentional about using discussion skills such as paraphrasing and waiting is Fishbowl. It begins with a small group of six to eight students sitting in an inner circle, with classmates circled around them. Those in the inner circle, because they are in a "fishbowl" being observed by others, tend to be more intentional in using discussion skills and following the agreed-upon procedures. Using processes to help students think about what they believe—and why—helps students learn to think about their thinking and be able to express their ideas. Processes that can be used for this purpose are described in Resource A.

Scaffold Discussion Skills With Feedback and Assessment

How did this discussion work and why? a teacher might ask after engaging small groups or the entire class in discussion. Some teachers work with students to create a rubric for discussion and ask students to assess themselves and the small group in which they participated. Possible topics for use in such an assessment appear in Figure 5.5.

Figure 5.5 Assessment of Discussion

Evidence of communication skills	Student comments relate to the topic.
	Students provide evidence for their statements.
	Students make eye contact with those listening.
	The voice modulates, demonstrating enthusiasm and authenticity.
Evidence of listening	Eye contact is made with those who speak.
	Body language demonstrates interest and understanding.
	Students honor think times.
	Students paraphrase peer comments accurately.
Evidence of accountability	All students participated.
	If a student didn't participate, someone asked her opinion.
	Students identified inconsistencies.
	Students asked peers for evidence in appropriate ways.

An important component of scaffolding discussion skills involves the teacher assessing the group's skills and providing feedback. When a problem area is identified, the teacher can provide extra practice in that area. Or the group may decide to appoint a monitor to collect more data about that specific skill. When one or more strengths are identified, students should be asked to give specific examples.

Expand Discussion Beyond the Classroom

Today's technology enables students to engage in discussion beyond the walls of the classroom. They can interact with others—across the state, country, or world—through blogs and wikis. How do students in London view a particular Shakespearian sonnet? How do students in Germany view the war in Iraq? How do students in China view the current economic situation? What is the understanding of global warming in Costa Rica or in Iceland? Once students know protocols for discussion, they can use these protocols to better understand the points of view of students from around the world.

Thinking Through QQ: Which of these ideas might you use to introduce or improve collaborative discussions in your classes? How would you go about presenting these ideas to your students?

CONNECTIONS: DEVELOPING LEARNER CAPACITY

Teachers can help build student capacity to develop response-ability for learning in the four ways presented in this chapter: (1) hold students accountable, (2) develop student capacity to ask quality questions, (3) provide opportunities for students to learn collaboratively, and (4) teach skills of collaborative discussion. To accomplish this, teachers can use a variety of structures and protocols that build the capacity of students to respond, ask questions, work collaboratively, and discuss skillfully. They can help students understand what good learning looks like, and they can engage students in actively creating a classroom where these behaviors are happening. It is not by accident that students learn to be response-able for their learning. Classroom practices that address metacognition, student engagement, and self-efficacy are required to develop response-ability among students.

Student Metacognition

- **What am I seeking to learn or be able to do?** Response-able learners engage fully in the process of learning and thinking; they can clearly articulate learning goals. If they understand the value of asking questions, they will clarify their own learning goals by asking, *What do I want to know?* and, *What do I want to be able to do?* In cooperative groups, students work collaboratively to formulate goals.

- **What do I currently know or think about the topic? Is it accurate?** In classrooms where every student is expected to formulate an answer, students will have an answer in mind and will be able to evaluate their responses in comparison to others' responses. This is a good beginning in helping them identify what they know, what they think they know, and what they want to learn about a given topic. As students ask questions about a topic, they will search for answers and will be able to determine what they know. Small-group discussion allows students to get a clear fix on the accuracy of the ideas they have about a given topic as they prepare to explore it further.

- **How will I make personal meaning of this content?** When students ask content-related questions, they are demonstrating that they are connecting the content to what they already know and are making meaning sufficiently to think about it, speculate, wonder, and hypothesize. In addition, collaborative group work helps students make personal meaning of content, as does the use of skillful discussion. As students listen respectfully to other students, they learn that many perspectives exist about a given topic. As they present their own ideas and search for evidence that these ideas are valid, they clarify their thinking and connect it to ideas they already have.

- **How am I monitoring my learning and progress?** As students become more sophisticated about the relationship between thinking and learning, they are in a better position to assess their learning and how close they are to attainment of their learning goals. The development of response-ability helps them take this monitoring seriously. Because they own their learning, they are able to self-assess. Their learning product is measured by themselves, not merely in accordance with what the teacher wants.

- **To what extent am I developing response-ability?** Throughout this chapter, we have looked at ways that students can be helped to develop an attitude of self-efficacy and of response-ability for their learning. As they live up to teacher expectations to answer all questions, formulate and pose questions, work with others collaboratively, and discuss in a skillful way, they are demonstrating that they believe they are responsible for their own learning.

- **What have I learned? How can I take my learning to the next level?** Response-able students are assessing their learning and own it.

Questions come to them about what they have learned, and these questions move them further in their exploration of a given skill or content area. Response-able students, through discussion of authentic ideas relevant to their lives, use technology to expand the community with whom they learn. No longer are assignments designed only by the teacher; students have input into the creation of projects that will take them further in their learning.

Student Engagement

Each of the behaviors discussed in this chapter stimulates student engagement. The use of alternative response formats engages students in thinking about questions and formulating responses. The posing of questions by students is a signal that engagement and thinking are high. Collaborative learning has been demonstrated to engage students more than most other instructional strategies. And finally, discussion serves to help students apply content at a personal level, engaging them fully.

When we think of the three components of the instructional core—and their relationships to one another—we can see that student response-ability changes the relationship between (1) teacher and student (as the teacher becomes less in control and the student takes more ownership) and (2) student and content (as students become more engaged with content on a personal level).

Student Self-Efficacy

Student self-efficacy increases as students take ownership of their learning. Response-able students are developing the capacity to set goals for their learning, to assess their prior knowledge in order to understand what they need to focus on, and to formatively assess their learning as they learn. They use these capacities to improve their learning, to pose quality questions that further their learning, and to interact with others in order to learn more.

- Imagine the sense of satisfaction when a student poses a question that the teacher cannot (or does not) answer but which the entire class undertakes to study!
- Imagine the sense of accountability when a student contributes (perhaps for the first time) to a class discussion and others acknowledge the importance of his insight!
- Imagine the sense of community when students contribute to their group's understanding of a complex problem on which the class has been working!

6

Create a Culture for Thinking

How Can You Use Quality Questioning to Create a Classroom Culture Where Students and Teacher Work Together to Advance Thinking and Knowing?

FOCUS QUESTIONS

1. How do you define a culture of thoughtfulness?

2. How do roles and relationships help define a culture?

3. Why is it important to actively teach norms for thinking through quality questioning?

4. What is the value of a language of thinking in creating a culture of thoughtfulness?

5. How do you define habits of mind? Which habits of mind underpin thinking and questioning?

6. What form can celebrations of questioning and thinking take in classrooms that are building thoughtful cultures?

> *To talk about a classroom culture for thinking is to talk about a classroom environment in which several forces—language, values, expectations, and habits—work together to express and reinforce the enterprise of good thinking.*
>
> —Shari Tishman,
> David N. Perkins, & Eileen Jay (1995, p. 2)

T homas Sergiovanni (2005), a thought leader in education leadership, refers to culture as "the normative glue" that holds a school together. Characterized by "shared visions, values, and beliefs at its core, culture serves as a compass setting, steering people in a common direction" (p. 1). The glue metaphor is no less appropriate for a classroom culture. If we are to create thoughtful classrooms, teachers and students need to be connected by a positive web of relationships based upon shared norms and habits of mind that value the process and outcomes of thinking.

Throughout this book, we introduce norms that underpin quality questioning and thinking. Norms, often described as "the way we do business around here," are the cornerstones of cultures. We cannot create classroom norms with a snap of our fingers or by posting them on a bulletin board. They evolve over time as individuals interact with and relate to one another. A teacher's success in gaining buy-in to preferred norms depends upon the quality of relationships among the targeted group. Like norms, relationships develop over time. So what does this mean for the creation of a classroom culture of thinking?

To create a culture, one must begin with a vision for what that culture should look like. Our vision for student thinking and learning appears in the opening of Chapter 1. Attainment of such a vision is always a work in progress, a never-ending endeavor. The building blocks for the vision are presented in Chapters 2 through 5, which focus on behaviors. These behaviors are associated with values and beliefs related to the vision.

As we were conceptualizing this book, there was no doubt that we would include a chapter on culture. The decision about where to position the chapter, however, was a difficult one. The question was whether to place it at the beginning or at the end of the book. Experience teaches that quality questioning and thinking behaviors cannot develop and blossom in a classroom devoid of a nurturing culture—so the temptation was to place it first. We know, however, that changes in beliefs follow changes in behaviors that lead to positive outcomes—hence, an argument can be made for placing it last, after the desired behaviors have been explicated. You are reading the answer to our question!

This chapter explores five behaviors associated with creating a culture for thinking:

- Develop collaborative, caring relationships
- Teach and reinforce norms for questioning and thinking

- Adopt a language of thinking
- Cultivate habits of mind
- Celebrate breakthroughs in thinking

As David Kobrin (2004) has observed (see quote), successful classroom leadership is shared among teacher and students. Likewise, teachers and students must share responsibility for these five behaviors if an authentic culture for thinking is to emerge.

DEVELOP COLLABORATIVE, CARING RELATIONSHIPS

Positive cultures begin and end with positive relationships. Positive, collaborative, and caring relationships are also the lifeblood of classroom cultures that nurture thinking. In Chapter 5, we linked student collaboration to improved student learning outcomes. We have repeatedly emphasized the importance of teachers communicating their interest in student answers, their commitment to student thinking, and their caring about student learning and growth. Throughout the book, we've focused on the importance of teachers working collaboratively to formulate quality questions, expecta-

> What does it mean to be the person in charge of a classroom? I like to think of teachers as leaders of small communities who bear responsibilities as overwhelming as those which face leaders of vast nation-states. To teachers falls the task of creating a classroom environment that promotes growth, learning, and understanding for all. Yet that's not a job one person can manage alone. Fortunately, every classroom has plenty of potential help: the students. The problem is marshaling the kids to the cause. . . . Classroom leadership depends on evoking willing participation from the kids in the room.
>
> —Kobrin (2004, p. 1)

tions for student responses, and potential scaffolds, and to reflect on their use of alternative questioning strategies and the results for students. All of these behaviors involve different roles and relationships than those found in traditional teacher-centered classrooms, in which control and compliance influence teacher-student and even student-student relationships.

Thinking Through QQ: What beliefs and values do you associate with collaborative, caring relationships? Jot these down in the margin. Now, compare them with our list in Figure 6.1. Have you identified beliefs that we omitted? If so, add them to the chart. Did you omit any that appear in this chart? Would you like to cultivate those in your classroom?

Figure 6.1 Beliefs and Values Associated With Collaborative, Caring Relationships

Belief/Value	Impact on Questioning and Thinking
1. Trust	Students are more likely to give and receive assistance (e.g., Use teacher scaffolding to reflect and continue thinking).
2. Respect	Students listen to one another—and to the teacher! They value diverse points of view.
3. Confidence	Students are willing to speak up and contribute in both small collaborative groups and whole-class interactions.
4. Security	Students are willing to take chances; they are not afraid to experiment, offer hypotheses, or ask questions.
5. Interdependence	Students understand that all of us know more than any one of us, and they willingly give and receive assistance.
6. Empathy	Students seek to understand where their peers are coming from and support them when they are discouraged.
7. Motivation	Student motivation increases when students know that their teacher and peers care whether they know and learn.

Later in this chapter, we will explore habits of mind that are associated with thoughtfulness. Because they contribute to both skillful thinking and positive relationships, some of these habits appear on this list as well. They are what we call power beliefs.

How can teachers go about reinforcing these beliefs in their class-rooms? We are guessing that you know your answer to this question and work with each new group of students to instill these beliefs. If you are like us, and like most other teachers who share these values, you use a variety of strategies to weave them into the fabric of your classroom culture, including (1) intentional and consistent modeling; (2) conversations with students about these beliefs, conducted in a systematic and routine man-ner (i.e., at the beginning of the school year, whenever a particular curricu-lar topic opens a door, and when special occasions or incidents present an opportunity); and (3) reinforcement of behaviors that exemplify the beliefs. If beliefs associated with caring, collaborative classrooms are already part of your classroom culture, you have a strong foundation on which to build relationships that support a culture of thoughtfulness.

When we say we consider relationships essential to a culture of thoughtfulness, we are including teacher-student, student-student, and teacher-teacher relationships. Although all three types of relationships are connected in many ways and influence one another in other manners, here, we will examine them one at a time.

Let's begin with teacher-student relationships that are collaborative and caring in nature and that nourish the culture we are imagining. First and foremost, we, as teachers, need to define the relationship as a partnership in learning, and we need to convey this to students in word and in deed. If we insist upon retaining our command-and-control role in the classroom, we cannot expect students to take ownership for their learning and become the kind of self-regulated learners we described earlier. This is a huge shift for many of us. Consider the changes highlighted in Figure 6.2.

As we cultivate learning partnerships with our students, we model the collaborative relationships we expect them to develop one with

Figure 6.2 Shifts in Teacher Role and Relationships With Students

From Command and Control	To Partner in Learning
Is the expert, the fount of all knowledge	Possesses expertise, but also serves as a coach and a resource broker for students; seeks to develop expertise in students
Establishes learning goals for the class that apply to all students	Expects students to form their own learning targets and assists them in doing so
Asks questions in order to get correct answers—has the answer in mind before asking	Asks questions to find out what students know in order to assist them in meeting learning targets
Almost always evaluates student answers and work products	Engages students in self-assessments and in peer assessments
Does a lot of telling or lecturing	Designs work for students that engages them in inquiry and discovery
Conducts class discussions in traditional manner—poses question; calls upon a student whose hand is raised; responds to that student, then calls on another; almost always comments after each student's response	Usually sits among students during a discussion, poses a question for discussion and invites students to interact with one another, asks questions only when curious or confused, and occasionally joins in with a comment
Tends to favor high-achieving students during class interactions by giving them more airtime during discussions, providing them with more wait time, more useful feedback, and so forth	Holds high expectations for all students, making all students accountable for knowing and responding in class; provides all students with equitable opportunities for responding

Figure 6.3 Shifts in Student Role and Relationships One With Another

From Individual Competitors	To Partners in Learning
Usually works alone and in isolation from classmates	Often is part of a learning team whose members work together to solve problems
Competes with classmates to get the best grades in class (or decides not to play the game)	Supports peers as all class members seek to attain learning targets and achieve mastery
Usually does not listen actively to classmates—listens only to the teacher, whose answers are the keys to good grades	Listens actively to classmates because the teacher values the insights of students and does not repeat student answers
Often fails to demonstrate respect for differing points of view	Listens to understand the perspectives of classmates who have different ways of viewing topics
Asks the teacher for help when a question or problem arises—rarely requests assistance from classmates	Turns to classmates with questions and requests for assistance—provides help to peers as needed

another. The idea is to develop a community of learners where students feel responsible not just for their own learning but also for their classmates' learning. This represents a sea change from the student-to-student relationship in traditional classrooms that is more competitive than collaborative in nature. Figure 6.3 contrasts the partnership with the competitive relationship.

Not only do teachers model partnership relationships with their students; they also do so with their peers. Students take notice when teachers collaborate with and learn from one another. We encourage teachers to find a peer partner who is willing to observe their classrooms for specific purposes and provide them with formative feedback and opportunities for reflection. Teachers who work in partnerships report that their students are very interested in the fact that their teachers are interested in learning and improving and that teachers work together toward this end. Students also know when they have assignments (and questions) similar to those of their peers in other classrooms; they know that teachers are talking and working together.

Classroom teachers have special opportunities for collaboration with inclusion and English as a second language (ESL) teachers who work with special populations in their classrooms. Again, students know if the professionals work as partners—that is, if teachers engage in shared inquiry to improve learning for targeted students. They also notice if the regular teacher assumes a proprietary attitude about the classroom.

The goal in a thoughtful classroom is to create a web of relationships that reflects a variety of partnerships in thinking and learning. Carefully crafted norms support the relationships we've outlined earlier.

Thinking Through QQ: Shifts in roles and relationships are necessary to the creation of a culture for thinking. Do you agree or disagree with this statement? Defend your answer.

TEACH AND REINFORCE NORMS FOR QUESTIONING AND THINKING

In each of the preceding chapters, we offered specific norms to support suggested behavior changes. We need to be clear: The mere posting of such statements in classrooms is not sufficient for their becoming authentic norms. Particularly in a community of learners, members must accept norm statements as guiding principles for their beliefs and behaviors. Norms that shape a culture for thinking require a different kind of buy-in from students than rules and procedures designed for purposes of classroom management.

If norms are to be truly effective, students as well as teachers must embrace them. This does not happen automatically; rather, teachers must design a plan that includes (1) presentation of each norm to students, (2) opportunities for student reflection about the meaning of the norm and its implications for their beliefs and behaviors, and (3) periodic review and refocusing on the norm. One model for teaching norms to students comes from Merrill Harmin (1994), who advocates truth signs, which he conceives of as "posted signs that remind students of important truths about learning and living" (p. 49). Harmin differentiates truth signs from classroom rules that tell students what to do. He offers the following as an example: "Everyone needs time to think and learn" (p. 49). Does this sound familiar?

Harmin also suggests that teachers introduce these statements one at a time over the course of the first several weeks of a new school term. We agree with Harmin that it is not enough to post these signs; we need to spend time in conversation with students helping them understand the *what* and the *why* of norms for thinking. Let's consider one of the norms we introduced in Chapter 3: Use teacher questions to prompt your thinking, not to guess the teacher's answer.

Perhaps the simplest and most direct way to help students understand a norm is to engage them in a discussion about it. Imagine the beginning of a school term with a class of fifth graders. Mr. Fernandez, a teacher in a self-contained classroom, is committed to introducing norms for questioning and thinking to his new students. What follows is the conversation he has with them about the norm related to the importance of their thinking of their own answers to his questions, as opposed to trying to figure out what he, the teacher, has in his mind.

Mr. Fernandez:	"I mentioned to you yesterday that we're going to talk about beliefs and behaviors that support our learning and thinking throughout our year together. Today I want you to reflect on this statement: Use teacher questions to prompt your thinking, not to guess the teacher's answer." (He points to a sentence strip on the classroom wall where he has posted the written statement.) "I'd like each of you to read this statement to yourselves and think about what it says to you." (He pauses for 30 seconds to give students time to reflect.) "Now, turn to your partner and share your thoughts about this statement." (He provides three minutes for student sharing.)
Mr. Fernandez:	"Now I'd like to hear from some of you." (He pauses for three seconds.) "What did you and Alicia have to say about the meaning of this norm, Marty?"
Marty:	"Well, I said it means that we should say what we are thinking, not what we think you are thinking." (three-second pause) "And Alicia said that she guesses that's what it means. But we both think that teachers want to hear right answers when they ask questions, so I guess we're kind of confused."
Mark:	"I think Mr. Fernandez is interested in correct answers, but I think he's saying we need to think of our best answer and say it, even if we are not sure."
Mr. Fernandez:	(nodding) "You're right, Mark. I do want you all to take your best crack at answering a question, but I want you to be thinking about what *you* know about the topic. I want you to focus on that, and then form your answer. I don't want you worrying about what I want you to say."
Mr. Fernandez:	"Now, think about why we would need this norm for our classroom community. Speculate as to why I would make such a deal out of this?" (pause) "OK. What is your theory, Kate?"
Kate:	"Uh . . . let me think. Oh, one thing I know is that most teachers don't seem to be asking us what we think; they

seem to call on the person who raises their hand to show they have the answer and want to say it. Maybe you want us to know that it will be different in this class."

| Mr. Fernandez: | "That's interesting, Kate, and you said just what I would have said. I remember when I was still in school, and I did just what you said. I raised my hand if I thought I had the teacher's answer. Last summer, though, I did some reading and thinking and I came to this conclusion: Usually, before I even ask students a question in class, I already have my answer to the question. In other words, I already know what I know and what I think. But I decided that questions really ought to be about what you know and what you think. Does that make sense to everyone?" |

| Joe: | "Yes, I think it makes sense, but I know it's going to be hard for me to answer if I'm not sure." |

| Mr. Fernandez: | "Well, Joe, I'll be waiting for your answer. See this norm?" (He points to another posted statement.) "Use the pause following the asking of a question to think and to formulate your response. This is about a concept called Wait Time 1, which is the time I'll wait after asking a question before calling on someone to answer. This is one of the think times we'll be giving one another. There's another time I'll be waiting for you to think, and that's after you stop talking when giving an answer. I'll usually wait three to five seconds after your last word before I say anything. The norm that addresses this is *Use the pause after your answer to reflect and add to or change it*. We'll be talking more about these two norms tomorrow. So stay tuned. Meanwhile, summarize what we've said today about the importance of your thinking of your own answers to my questions. Cynthia?" |

| Cynthia: | "Well, we've been talking about the fact that you already know the answers to your own questions, so you want us to think of what *we* know and think when you pose questions—and not worry about *your* answer." |

| Mr. Fernandez: | "Thank you, Cynthia. Thumbs up if you agree with Cynthia. Thumbs to the side if you are not sure." (pause) "Good, I see all thumbs up, and I'm going to expect to hear a lot of your good thinking this year." |

We suggest that you have a similar conversation with students about all of the norms that you select to support thinking and questioning. We also recommend that you consider another strategy advocated by Harmin (1994), that of cushioning, which he defines as questions or statements intended to reinforce norms (p. 56). For example, imagine you are in Mr. Fernandez's class one week after the previous interchange. On that day, he plans to facilitate a whole-class discussion in which he'll be posing one to three focusing questions intended to lead his students into critical analysis and evaluation of a novel they have been reading together. He wants to remind them of the importance of voicing their own ideas:

Mr. Fernandez:	"Today, you'll have an opportunity to serve as book critics. I will pose a few questions that I want you to think about individually. Then, we'll follow our protocol for discussion to surface your ideas about the novel we've read together."
	"Before beginning, I want you to look around the room at the norms we have posted, and decide which of these will be important to the success of our discussion." (He pauses a minute or so to give students a chance to review the norms.)
	"Which of our norms suggests that you should contribute your own ideas to our conversation?" (three-second pause) "Tony?"
Tony:	"I think there are at least two that will help here." (He looks at the posted norm.) "*Use teacher questions to prompt your thinking, not to guess the teacher's answer*, and *use the pause following the asking of a question to think and to formulate your response.*"
Mr. Fernandez:	"I agree with Tony. How many of you selected these norms? Show me thumbs up if you did." (pause) "I think we have consensus. I am interested in why you think it's important not to spend your time guessing my answer." (pauses) "Alonzo, what are you thinking?"
Alonzo:	"I think it allows me to focus on what I really think when I don't have to worry about your opinion."

Cushioning reminds students of the norms and connects them to the here-and-now classroom situations in which they can be most powerful. Harmin (1994) suggests that teachers employ the cushioning strategy daily to reinforce the importance of one or more shared norms for thinking and learning. In his view, when students feel secure about the ways in which classroom interactions will proceed, their "natural curiosities are freed," and they are better able to participate in "a classroom of active learning" (p. 61).

Thinking Through QQ: Figure 6.4 displays all of the norms introduced in connection with *Thinking Through Quality Questioning.* These are the authors' norms; we want you to think critically about the norms that will help you accomplish the goals *you* have for *your* students. You may choose some of the norms listed here; you may add others. You may reword to make them meaningful to your students, given their age, grade level, and other characteristics. Read our norms, critically evaluate them, and decide which you would like to use as a beginning point for the set of norms you desire for your classroom.

When all members of a learning community share these kinds of norms, a synergy emerges, as well as a press for questioning and thinking. Individual students who might not be disposed to thinking come under the influence of others in the classroom. Thought leaders of Harvard University's Project Zero express it this way: "The idea of a culturally supportive environment is that you see good thinking all around you because

Figure 6.4   Norms Associated With Thinking Through Quality Questioning

Purposes of Questioning
Use teacher questions to prompt your thinking, not to guess the teacher's answer.
Use mistakes as opportunities to learn: This is a risk-free classroom.
Use follow-up questions to think about and self-assess your first response and to modify or extend your thinking.
Be open to wonder and ask, not just to know and answer.
Wait Times
Use the pause following the asking of a question to think and to formulate your response.
Use the pause after your answer to reflect and add to or change it.
Use the pause following a classmate's answer to compare it with your own. Be ready to agree or disagree and to add your ideas.
Participation
Listen with respect to other points of view in order to fully understand and learn.
Share what you think so others can learn from you.
Monitor your talk so others can contribute.

everybody is doing it. . . . It involves infusing values and norms into the culture and building expectations for good thinking" (Tishman, Perkins, & Jay, 1995, p. 49).

ADOPT A LANGUAGE OF THINKING

Analyze. Classify. Contrast. Hypothesize. Infer. Predict. Speculate. These are all strong thinking verbs, words that thought leaders in the field associate with classroom cultures that incorporate a language of thinking (Costa & Kallick, 2000, pp. 15–33; Perkins, 1992, pp. 107–110; Swartz, Costa, Beyer, Reagan, & Kallick, 2008, p. 85; Tishman et al., 1995, pp. 15–33). Likewise, there are nouns that resound in a classroom where thinking thrives: *assumption, criteria for judgment, consequences, data, evidence, reasoning, results,* and so forth.

A language of thinking promotes exactness and precision in expressing cognitive processing. The importance of oral language to learning permeates the thinking of the giants of educational theory, including Piaget, Vygotsky, and Feuerstein. These eminent researchers affirmed: "Oral language helps direct [students'] thinking processes. The fewer opportunities students have to verbalize and refine their thoughts, the less they can develop clear thought patterns allowing them to become independent, lifelong learners" (Hopkins, 2010, p. 83). When students learn the vocabulary of thinking, they are better able to communicate their thinking so as to make it visible to others in their learning community.

The cognitive processing matrix associated with the Revised Bloom Taxonomy (Anderson & Krathwohl, 2001; see Figure 2.3 in Chapter 2) is a good source for selecting words to incorporate into your classroom's language of thinking. Many teachers with whom we have worked use a word wall to display vocabulary associated with thinking. They are intentional in teaching students the meaning of the thinking words and of incorporating them into their daily talk. Additionally, they encourage students to use thinking verbs and nouns to express the manner in which they are processing information.

> To achieve thoughtful learning, we need to create a culture of thoughtful learning in the classroom. This is a matter of how teachers talk to students, students to teachers, and students to one another. And talk here is of course a matter not just of the words used but of manner and style and goals.
>
> —Perkins (1992, p. 112)

We advance thinking not only through use of precise vocabulary, but also by selecting particular modes of expression, namely, by posing questions rather than enunciating facts or opinions. Francis Hunkins (1995), a longtime student of questioning for thinking, advocates the use of questions as a "language of possibility" and argues that "viewing questions as part of a language of possibility allows both teachers and students to realize that thinking, reflecting, [and] participating in making meaning is a human process. . . . Questions additionally serve as the building blocks for creating realities. As part of a language of possibility, questions allow discoveries [and] enable inventions [and] creations" (p. 144). The language of possibility oftentimes begins with such stems as *What if . . . ? I wonder what might happen . . . Can you imagine . . . ?* and *What are the implications of . . . ?*

Thinking Through QQ: Imagine that you've helped each student in your class develop a language of thinking. What kinds of changes would you expect in class discussions and other interactions?

CULTIVATE HABITS OF MIND

Earlier in this chapter, we argued for infusing norms for questioning and thinking into the classroom culture. Norms regulate interactions between individuals and within groups. Another set of value-laden guidelines supporting thinking is called habits of mind by some (Costa & Kallick, 2000; Swartz et al., 2008, pp. 17–22) and thinking dispositions by others (Ritchhart & Perkins, 2005, pp. 785–789; Tishman et al., 1995, pp. 56–64). John Dewey emphasized the "importance of good habits of mind that carry people past moments of distraction and reluctance" (Dewey quoted by Ritchhart & Perkins, 2005, p. 785).

> Good thinkers, after all, are more than people who simply think well when they think: They also think at the right times with the right commitments—to truth and evidence, creativity and perspective taking, sound decisions, and apt solutions. Views of thinking that bring this to the fore are often called *dispositional* because they look not just to how well people think when trying hard but to what kinds of thinking they are *disposed* to undertake.
>
> —Ritchhart & Perkins (2005, p. 785)

Thinking through quality questioning incorporates habits of mind and thinking dispositions that include these shared characteristics:

- They positively impact all kinds of thinking.
- Like all habits, they evolve over time; however, when in place, they become automatic.
- Teachers can actively model and directly teach these dispositions.
- They motivate individuals to be thoughtful.
- A culture for thinking reinforces these habits or dispositions; in turn, they strengthen the thinking culture.

Although there are some slight differences in experts' lists of these habits or dispositions, those named in Figure 6.5 are included across all such lists that we have examined.

Figure 6.5 Habits of Mind or Thinking Dispositions That Support Thinking Through Quality Questioning

Habit of Mind/Disposition	What It Looks Like in a Classroom
Pursuit of *Accuracy*	Students seek evidence to support their conclusions. They reflect on their thinking to self-assess and self-correct.
Intellectual *Curiosity*	Students ask *what-if* questions. They want to know why, not just what.
Empathetic *Listening*	Students listen to understand others' points of view. They look at the speaker with interest, think about what he is saying, and question to get behind what they may not at first understand.
Flexibility in Thinking	Students are willing to try out different types of thinking and different points of view.
Managing Impulsivity	Students think before speaking. They suspend judgment and reflect on their initial reactions. They seek to uncover all of the evidence as well as to hear a speaker's reasoning to its culmination.
Open-Mindedness	Students ask questions with real interest in another's point of view. They are open to continual learning about a topic.
Perseverance or Persistence	Students do not give up when confronting a difficult challenge; rather, they redouble their efforts and look to outside resources for assistance.
Taking *Reasonable Risks*	Students are adventuresome in their thinking. They are willing to move outside of the bounds of certainty to offer a new solution to a problem or introduce a new topic for investigation. They are not afraid to venture into new territories of thinking and learning.
Reflection	Students value time to think about their learning, their thinking, and their work products. They also reflect on the broader meaning of a subject of study, seeking relevance to their lives outside of the classroom.

Remember, the list of habits and dispositions presented in Figure 6.5 is not exhaustive. You may identify others that you believe to be of critical importance to your students and your classroom. As you reflect on and select habits of mind, be certain that they are habits that you own or that you are willing to cultivate. We cannot teach our students habits that we ourselves do not possess.

Beliefs about how learning occurs and beliefs about one's own cognitive abilities affect an individual's readiness to develop a particular habit of mind. For example, Carol Dweck (2006, pp. 6–7), a Stanford University professor, distinguishes between individuals who possess a fixed mind-set and those who choose a growth mind-set. Those with fixed mind-sets believe that their abilities are carved in stone, that their intelligence, personality, and other personal traits are givens. On the other hand, those with growth mind-sets consider change to be possible through hard work and experience. Dweck's research reveals that people with a fixed mind-set are unlikely to adopt perseverance or persistence when they confront a challenging thinking task; rather, they tend to quit. Those with a growth mind-set, however, believe that a step-by-step approach can lead to success. Other researchers have found that these traits or mind-sets are "independent of cognitive abilities but often affect cognitive performance greatly" (Ritchhart & Perkins, 2005, p. 786). The lesson for teachers appears to be twofold: (1) help students chunk out large tasks into smaller increments so that they can experience success step-by-step, and (2) seek to model and actively teach the value of perseverance in thinking.

Thinking Through QQ: Reflect individually or talk with a colleague about how you might use habits of mind to foster a growth mind-set among your students.

CELEBRATE BREAKTHROUGHS IN THINKING

Terry Deal and Kent Peterson's (2009) model for a strong culture includes vision, norms, rituals and traditions, and celebrations. Each of these components of culture is important, and each is addressed in this book. Chapter 1 presents a vision for a culture of thinking. Related norms are presented throughout Chapters 3, 4, and 5. Teachers can tap into each chapter in the book to identify processes they may wish to morph into rituals and traditions. Examples include use of the Revised Bloom Taxonomy (Anderson & Krathwohl, 2001) to challenge students to higher levels of thinking, graphic organizers to make thinking visible, or exit passes to prompt student summaries of daily thinking. In this final section, we suggest ways that we can celebrate student thinking so as to continue the motivation and momentum required to energize and revitalize a classroom culture for thinking.

Deal and Peterson (2009) cite research to argue that continuous improvement is most likely to occur when "small successes are recognized and celebrated through shared ceremonies commemorating both individual and group contributions" (p. 11). They view celebrations as the fuel that keeps the fire of improvement blazing. We believe that creating a culture for thinking will always be a work in progress for teachers. Each day brings new challenges, and each year brings new students. We cannot rest on our laurels when it comes to culture-building.

So what types of celebrations are appropriate to celebrate thinking and questioning? Certainly, this depends upon multiple variables, including teachers' own personalities and what seems right to them, the ages and grade levels of their students, the personalities and other traits of their students, and the school culture within which they work. For that reason, this book does not provide a prescription for the right forms of celebration for you to use in your classroom. In order to be meaningful, however, celebrations must honor authentic achievements that are tied to individual and classroom goals for thinking and learning.

As teachers, we can facilitate the identification of classroom goals for thinking. These goals can focus on thinking outcomes and/or thinking dispositions. The important thing is that we assist the class as a whole in setting these goals. Likewise, as part of their metacognitive work, we can help individual students set their own thinking goals. Important for both classroom and individual goals are monitoring and making visible incremental progress toward these goals. As individual students and the class at large attain important milestones, we can stop and acknowledge the moment. The celebration does not need to be elaborate. It may be no more than a pause in our journey toward thinking through quality questioning.

THE ENDGAME

John Barell (1995) wrote a book titled *Teaching for Thoughtfulness*, which is a longtime favorite of ours. Barell conceives of thoughtfulness in both senses of the word: teaching students to think and encouraging them to be considerate and respectful one of another. Like Barell, we believe that these two types of thoughtfulness reinforce and support one another. When students adopt the norms and habits of mind associated with thinking, they commit to respect and care about one another's thinking and learning. In turn, if they respect and care about one another, they will listen in order to understand and think before they speak. We have attempted to paint a picture of a culture for thinking and learning that radiates this thoughtfulness.

Each of the previous chapters in this book concludes with a synthesis piece that relates a component of the Framework for Thinking Through Quality Questioning to student metacognition, engagement, and self-efficacy. We make the case that quality questioning, in addition to driving learning and thinking, promotes these three important variables for developing independent and responsible learners. However, in order for these three components to be addressed through quality questioning, students must have trusting and respectful relationships with their peers and their teachers. They need to feel that their learning is important to others and that their thinking and contributions to their classroom communities are valued. Teachers who value student thinking and believe it to be the key to learning and achievement will cocreate with their students a culture of thoughtfulness, which nurtures quality questioning for all.

Thinking Through QQ: To what extent do you believe you are currently *teaching for thoughtfulness*? What steps can you take to be more intentional in this endeavor? What kinds of conversations can you imagine having with your students?

Resource A

*Processes to Engage
Learners in Thinking*

Affinity Mapping

Data on Display

Final Word

Fishbowl

Ink Think (nonverbal mind mapping)

Interview Design

IQ Pairs

Jigsaw

KQS × 3

KWL

Peoplegraph

Questioning Circle

Question, Question

Round-Robin Questioning

Say Something

Synectics

Table Rounds

Thinkathon

Think-Pair-Share

Tuning Protocol

AFFINITY MAPPING

Purpose: Engages students in analyzing data to identify relationships and create conceptual categories.

Preparation: Prepare a question that will generate many responses from students. Provide each student with sticky notes and a pen or pencil. Provide each group of students with a large piece of paper (e.g., butcher, flip chart, or poster board).

Facilitation: Ask students to respond to the question (individually or in pairs) by writing each response on a separate sticky note. After allowing sufficient time for generating ideas, ask each group to silently post its sticky notes on a large piece of paper. Direct them to look for related ideas and to form clusters of sticky notes. Ideas can be grouped and regrouped by any member of the team, as each looks for commonalities among ideas. Sticky notes can be moved numerous times until group members feel satisfied that they have created meaningful concepts or clusters of ideas. As a last task, each group should name each cluster of ideas. As groups share with the larger class, look for how many groups came up with similar categories. Did they find different ways to consolidate ideas?

Sample Questions

- History: What have been the main causes of conflict between countries?
- Mathematics: How do we use fractions in everyday life?
- Metacognition: How do you learn best?

DATA ON DISPLAY

Purpose: Helps establish a risk-free environment in which students engage in discussion based on data—not on their own ideas, assumptions, and opinions. The process promotes individual reflection, equitable contributions from all class members, and analysis of a visual display of the thinking of the whole group (see Illustration A.1). The process moves students from thinking about their own ideas to thinking about implications of the responses from the entire class. Data on Display prompts student questions, conclusions, hypothesis formulation, and examination of their own and others' assumptions.

Preparation: Select a topic, and prepare four to six statements about which students can agree or disagree. For best results, the statements will create cognitive dissonance (e.g., pose a belief statement with which students might strongly agree, followed by a statement of action that does not align with the belief). Prepare a handout for each student on which each statement appears with a scale from 100 to 0. In addition, write each question or statement at the top of a sheet of easel paper. Down the left edge of the chart, include a scale ranging from 100 to 0, marked off in 10-point increments. Leave enough space between the numbers for students to place sticky notes (see Illustration A.1). Give each student one sticky note (preferably 0.5" × 1.75") per question. Hang the charts around the room. For best results, seat students in small groups.

Illustration A.1 Data on Display

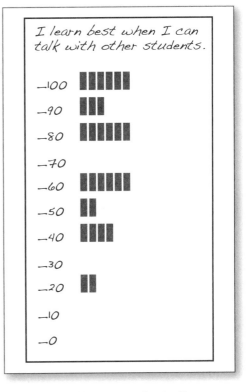

Facilitation: Ask students to individually select the extent to which they agree (from 0% to 100%) with each of the statements and to mark their responses on their handouts. Students then will post their responses/sticky notes on the appropriate charts, contributing to a bar graph for each statement. Allow time for individuals to view the charts and come to conclusions about what the data mean. Allow additional time for students to discuss the data in small groups. Finally, facilitate a whole-class discussion to identify conclusions and implications.

Modifications: For primary students, read each statement aloud. Instead of percentages, use signs such as a smiley face, a neutral face, and a frowny face. For elementary students, give four or five choices on a scale of 0 to 4 or 0 to 5.

Integration of math: Ask students to calculate an average or median response for each statement. Ask what fraction or percentage of the class answered at a given level or above a given level.

Thinking strategies: Ask students to speculate about why some students might have rated the same statement high and others low. Ask them to formulate hypotheses about how other students (older or younger) might answer these same questions. As students study the data, ask them to pose questions about what they see. What questions do they have about the data?

Sample Questions

English Literature

- It is always wrong to kill another person.
- Because the character in the book killed in self-defense, it was an acceptable action.
- I can think of times when someone might need to kill someone else—other than in self-defense.
- It is hard to say that something is "always wrong" or "always right" because it depends on circumstances.

Health

- When we eat properly, we are more mentally alert and we have more energy.
- Every morning, I eat a healthy breakfast before I come to school.
- The human body requires sufficient sleep to perform well.
- I go to bed early enough to assure that I get eight hours of sleep.

Metacognition

- I learn best when I can talk to other students.
- It helps me learn when I understand clearly what I am learning and why it is important.
- In most of my classes, I have the opportunity to talk to others about what we are learning.
- In most of my classes, what we are learning is relevant to me, and I understand the importance of the topic.

FINAL WORD

Purpose: Encourages listening to and learning from different points of view about a common reading; helps students think through, in depth, their own understanding of a specific passage of text; and facilitates true comprehension and meaning making. The use of this and other protocols will scaffold skills of discussion among students in the classroom. This protocol specifically helps students practice wait time because they speak only when it is their turn to speak. Students will also benefit by learning better how to listen to fully understand.

Preparation: Identify a common reading related to the topic under study. Ask students to read it before coming to class. Allow time, in class, for them to review the reading and to identify three ideas about which they would be willing to talk or hear discussion. Seat students in groups of four.

Facilitation: Ask each group to identify (1) a facilitator, who will monitor the group's use of the Final Word protocol; (2) a timekeeper, who will alert participants to the time; and (3) a volunteer, to go first in introducing an idea from the reading. Share a written copy of the instructions for the protocol, especially for the first use with a class.

Throughout this process, when one student is speaking, others in the group are quiet; they are listening or taking notes.

The first volunteer in the group selects one of his ideas, directs the attention of others in the group to the place in the reading where it appears, and talks about this idea for up to three minutes. When the first student finishes talking (or when time is called), each of the other group members will respond, in turn, for up to one minute each—staying on the topic introduced by the first student. When all group members have responded, the original speaker has up to one minute to give the final word on the topic. (For younger students, you may use shorter times and keep time for all groups.)

A second student then selects one of her ideas and follows the same process. If time allows, every student introduces an idea from the reading for discussion by the group.

Debrief the process with students by posing the following kinds of questions: *How did it feel to follow this protocol? What were the advantages to them of following this process? How did it affect their comprehension of the passage? What did they learn during the process—about the text and about their process of learning? How would you modify this process for the next time we use it?*

Adapted from the National School Reform Faculty (NSRF) at www.nsrfharmony.org. Other helpful text-based protocols from NSRF include the Four A's and Save the Last Word for Me.

FISHBOWL

Purpose: Engages a small group of students in true dialogue with one another, helps a group learn the skills of dialogue and be intentional in practicing them, and encourages active listening and questioning.

Preparation: Prepare a pivotal question around which a group might have varied opinions and engage in dialogue. Arrange chairs in two concentric circles, with 6 to 10 chairs in the inside circle and the remaining chairs in the outside circle.

Facilitation: Begin by sharing group norms such as these: have an open mind; listen with respect to others' responses, seeking to fully understand; use Wait Time 2, allowing at least three to five seconds of silence after each speaker; and monitor your participation, contributing ideas and allowing others to do the same.

Select a group of students to sit in the inner circle (or fishbowl). Add an empty chair in the inner circle. Direct other students to sit in the outer circle. Explain that the inside circle will model dialogue—clarifying assumptions, speaking without defensiveness, and working to understand others' points of view. The outer circle is to (1) listen to the exchange of ideas, (2) briefly join the inner circle by sitting in the empty chair to pose a question or make a statement (which pushes the thinking of the fishbowl members), and (3) monitor the use of norms and dialogic skills used by the members of the fishbowl.

Pose the pivotal question. Allow time for the group to respond. Prompt for clarification, as necessary; monitor the use of norms.

Debrief the process, first with the inner circle and then with the outer circle: *What did you learn during this experience? How did you feel? How did it prompt thinking?*

Tip: For a rich discussion, give the question or questions to small groups for discussion prior to the Fishbowl. Include a member from each small group in the inner circle; this will accomplish representation of ideas from the entire class. Alternatively, allow time for individuals to respond in writing to a prompt prior to entering the fishbowl discussion.

INK THINK

Purpose: Helps a group create information in a visual, nonlinear way; stimulates thinking; helps to develop new patterns of thought; and encourages students to go deeper in their thinking about a particular subject.

Preparation: Create a question that will prompt divergent student thinking about a topic under study. Prepare a wall chart and/or table space or a workstation for each group of 6 to 10 students. Put a word, phrase, or symbol in the center of the chart to represent what you want the group to think about. Provide a marker for each student.

Facilitation: Ask students to reflect on the question and to individually write their ideas. Encourage them to record all thoughts without monitoring, as in brainstorming. Then, have students work together in groups of 6 to 10. Before the groups move to their stations, explain that this activity is to be done *in silence.* Members of each small group are to "listen" to one another by silently reading what other group members write on the wall chart.

Ink Think is a group's nonverbal creation of a mind map. Main ideas are written on lines that emanate from the central idea; other ideas will branch off of these. As they gather at a chart, students will draw or write their responses on the paper. Often, they will read another's idea and will add details, examples, specificity, or related ideas.

Monitor as groups work. If necessary, remind students that Ink Think is to be done in silence. Allow adequate time for each group to record its ideas. After sufficient time, ask each group to prepare a summary to share with the larger group. Look for commonalities among groups as they report.

Modifications: You might create four or five related questions. In this event, ask students to reflect on all of them; assign one per group. When the groups have completed responding to their assigned questions, ask each group to rotate clockwise to another chart, read through the ideas, and add their thoughts to it. Continue until each group has recorded ideas about each question. Ask each group to summarize the responses to their original question and report major ideas to the class.

Sample Questions

Science

- What have been the benefits of the human genome project? What future benefits do you envision?
- How has science changed our lives since the beginning of the 20th century? How has it changed our ways of thinking?

Math

- How do you use geometry in your lives? How might you use it in the future?
- For what purposes do we use statistics? Why is it important to understand?

Social Studies

- In what ways did the transcontinental railroad change the United States?
- In what ways are your lives different today because of the Civil Rights legislation of the 1960s?

Metacognition

- What helps you think?
- How is thinking related to learning?

INTERVIEW DESIGN

Purpose: Engages all class members in asking and answering a set of questions in a one-on-one setting; students gather and summarize information and perceptions from other students in an equitable and risk-free manner. Provides practice in posing questions and in using quality-questioning strategies.

Preparation: Prepare four questions of equal complexity around the topic of interest. Label the questions A through D. Create a handout with each question written on the top; make enough copies so that a fourth of the class will get question A, a fourth will get question B, and so forth. Arrange the room so that there are several sets of eight chairs (a row of four facing a row of four), with enough chairs for all students.

Facilitation: The Interview Design process encompasses two phases.

Phase 1: The Interviews. After students are seated in the rows, review the process of interviewing:

- Ask with interest in the response.
- Use wait time.
- Record what is said.
- Probe, as necessary, to get behind the other's thinking (e.g., *Can you give an example? Can you say more about that?*).
- Refrain from making evaluative comments.

In each row of four chairs, assign each student one of the four questions, A through D; assign each student's partner (the person in the facing chair) the same question so that question A faces A, B faces B, and so forth.

Allow a few minutes for the partners to ask and answer their assigned question. Then, within each set of eight chairs, have one row of four participants remain seated while those in the facing row move in the following order: The person on one end of the moving row gets up and walks to the other end of the row, and the others in his row each move down one seat to let him sit in the end chair. Allow time for the new partners to ask one another their questions, and then have those in the moving row move again. Continue this pattern until every person in each row has answered all four questions—and has asked her question to each of the people in the facing row.

Phase 2: Summarizing Data. Students gather with others who asked the same question (all the A's in a group, all the B's in a group, etc.). As a group, they read the responses they collected and create a summary. One member of the group, the recorder, writes down the major ideas and shares results with the large group.

Tips

1. Provide context for each question by prefacing it with a statement or quote.

2. Use a timer and call time so that each person has the opportunity to pose a question and respond before the group moves.

3. Make accommodations, when the size of the group isn't evenly divisible by the number of questions, by adding a person to either end of one of the nonmoving rows.

4. After some experience with the interview process, have cooperative groups formulate a question to use during the process, collect data from peers, summarize their findings, and prepare a report to the rest of the class.

IQ PAIRS

Purpose: The Insight-Question (IQ) Pairs strategy engages students in pairs to talk about a short reading, quote, or question. This strategy prepares students for a large-group discussion by giving them an opportunity to identify and clarify their thoughts in a low-risk environment (pairs) before sharing in a larger group setting.

Preparation: Identify a short, thought-provoking passage, quote, or question. Have each student find a partner with whom to talk.

Facilitation: Display the passage, quote, or question so that all students can read it. Explain that after they read it, each student should share with his partner (1) an insight and (2) a question based on the passage.

After sufficient time for discussion in pairs, call on a student to share her partner's insight; move to hear from other partnerships as well.

JIGSAW

Purpose: Provides a structure for cooperative group learning, whereby students learn from one another. Encourages students to take responsibility for their own learning as each assumes the role of teacher for his small group.

Preparation: Identify a reading or several readings around which to organize Jigsaw. Create worksheets for each expert group. At a minimum, such worksheets should include the page numbers for the assigned reading, questions to think about and discuss with other members of the expert group, and suggestions for organizing a presentation to be made to the home groups.

Facilitation: Organize students into heterogeneous home groups. Describe the Jigsaw process and be sure that each student has an assignment.

(Note: If there are five different concepts or readings, home groups will be composed of five students, each of whom assumes a different assignment.) Like a jigsaw puzzle, in which every piece is necessary to complete the picture, the home group is composed of five students, each of whom becomes an expert on one portion of the assignment, learning with others in an expert group composed of other students with the same assignment. After learning, all students return to their home groups to teach other members. Without every member, the learning is incomplete.

As students begin in their home groups, distribute the readings and assign one to each student or allow each student to select her assignment. Ask students to reorganize so that they meet in expert groups (i.e., with other students who have the same assignment). They will read the assigned material as indicated on the worksheet; discuss questions, as outlined; and prepare to share their learning with others in their home groups. After sufficient time, students return to their original home groups in order to teach one another what they have learned.

Debrief the Process With the Class

- Did you like this method of learning? Why or why not?
- Did every member of your group assume responsibility for the group's learning? What is evidence of that responsibility?
- How would you improve this strategy?
- Did you learn more or less from other students compared with what you typically learn from the teacher? Why might this be?

KQS × 3

Purpose: As a metacognitive structure for students who are working on inquiry-based learning, Know, Question, Strategies (KQS) × 3 provides key questions to drive the planning, the investigation, and the assessment of a project.

Preparation: Hand out a worksheet (sample provided) to guide students engaged in inquiry-based learning.

Facilitation: As a subject is assigned or selected by students for study, direct them in cooperative groups to the top row of questions to guide their planning: What do we think we know about this subject? What questions will drive our inquiry? What strategies will we use to investigate and learn more about this topic? Once they have defined their question for study and they are in the middle of exploring their topic, suggest they visit the second row of questions: How are we extending and deepening our knowledge? What additional questions are emerging? What other strategies and resources do we need? Finally, as they wrap up their project, encourage them to assess their study by reflecting on the bottom row of questions: What new knowledge and understandings have we acquired? What other questions do we have? How can we strategically apply our new knowledge in other settings?

Planning		
K: What do we think we know about this subject?	Q: What questions will drive our inquiry?	S: What strategies will we use to investigate and learn more about this topic?
Investigating		
K: How are we extending and deepening our knowledge?	Q: What additional questions are emerging?	S: What other strategies and resources do we need?
Assessing		
K: What new knowledge and understandings have we acquired?	Q: What other questions do we have?	S: How can we strategically apply our new knowledge in other settings?

KWL

Purpose: The Know, Want to Know, Learned (KWL) process helps students assess their prior knowledge of a subject, identify items of interest and questions they have about a given topic, and self-assess what they have learned. In this process, often done as a class or in a collaborative group, students learn by hearing other students think aloud and process questions and information.

Preparation: None required.

Facilitation: Often teachers lead this process with the entire class. Alternately, it can be done by individual students or in collaborative groups. At the beginning of a unit or lesson, pose two questions:

1. What do you think you know about this topic? (K)

2. What do you want to learn about this topic? (W)

At the conclusion of a unit, revisit answers to the first two questions, letting students identify misconceptions they may have held before the study and any new questions they want to pursue about the topic. Then ask them to address a third question:

3. What have you learned about this topic? (L)

PEOPLEGRAPH

Purpose: Engages students in thinking about and clarifying their understanding of an issue under study prior to the topic being opened for large-group discussion.

Preparation: Formulate a statement that is central to an issue under study. In order to be appropriate for the Peoplegraph process, the statement should be one that promotes differing points of view—and one with which students can either agree or disagree. Prepare a handout with the statement and space for students to write their responses.

Facilitation: Ask students to think about the statement and to write individually about their beliefs. After a few minutes, ask them to determine the extent to which they agree or disagree with the statement and to be prepared to offer reasons for their position on the issue. Establish a continuum—an imaginary or real line in the classroom or hallway—with one end designated "strongly agree" and the opposite end designated "strongly disagree." Ask each student to "take a stand" at the point along the continuum that represents his current point of view on the statement. After students have taken a position, tell them to form a group with two or three others who are standing nearby. In these small groups, they will share their reasons for selecting the position they took along the Peoplegraph. After about five minutes, ask a spokesperson from one of the groups to offer reasons to support that group's position. Open the floor for comments from other groups.

Variations: This is a good strategy to use prior to a Fishbowl, where the discussion can move into dialogue, with students intentionally using active listening and other communication strategies to understand others' points of view. Some teachers like to group students with opposing views, having the *strongly disagree* end of the Peoplegraph get together with students from the *strongly agree* end to promote better understanding of opposing viewpoints.

Integration of math: After students have formed the Peoplegraph, ask them to create numerical equivalents to the student positions. For example, what percentage of students strongly agreed with the statement? What percentage held views similar to their own? What percentage was in the middle?

Developing thinking: What are the reasons that students have divergent views on this statement? What, in your background knowledge or experiences, influenced your stand on this statement? What might be the factors that influenced others' thinking? What questions do you have about this statement? Do you believe there is a right or wrong answer? By what criteria should we make judgments about the truth of this statement?

QUESTIONING CIRCLE

Purpose: Encourages question formulation, engages students in thinking about a reading in order to identify key ideas and formulate questions about them, facilitates listening to and learning from different points of view about a common reading, and helps students come to a deeper understanding—and make personal meaning—of a written passage.

Preparation: Before introducing this strategy, talk with students about the relationship between questioning and learning. Revisit the norm that encourages students to ask questions. Talk with students about what makes a question a quality question—one they want to think about and try to answer.

Identify a reading (an article or a chapter from a book on the content under study). Assign it for homework. Prepare written directions for the process.

Facilitation: Organize students into learning groups of four. Before you begin the process, ask each student individually to review the reading and identify three ideas that are interesting—ideas they would like to think about further. Tell students to mark these passages as they read so that they can easily find them later and direct peers to them. For each of these three ideas, students should craft an open-ended question. This should be a true question (one they truly wonder about), and it should call for responses that are above the level of remember.

Each group should identify (1) a facilitator, who will make sure that the group stays on task and that everyone participates, and (2) a volunteer to go first in posing one of her questions from the reading. During this entire process, as one person is speaking, *others in the group should be quiet* as they listen or take notes. This is not a discussion; in this protocol, there is no back-and-forth conversation, as is typical among discussions.

The first volunteer in the group selects one of his ideas, directs the attention of the group to the place in the reading where it can be found, and then poses his question. After some think time, the person to the right of the question-asker begins to address the question. Note: This is not so much to answer the question as it is to think aloud about the question, with the question-asker listening in. When the first person finishes talking, the others, in turn, have an opportunity to address the question posed by the first volunteer. Finally, after every member of the group has discussed the question, it returns to the original question-poser, who then can think aloud about his own question. This concludes the first round.

In turn, each of the other group members introduces a topic and poses a question, listens as the question is addressed by all group members, and then speaks about it. After all members have had an opportunity to pose a question, the cycle is complete.

Debrief this process with students: *How did the Questioning Circle strategy affect your understanding of the reading passage? Speculate as to what about the process might have affected your understanding. Did the prior formation of a question affect your listening to other group members talk about the topic? Speculate as to why or why not.*

Question for reflection: Were some questions more engaging than other questions? Did the question-engagement seem to differ by individual? What seemed to be the characteristics of the questions that were the most engaging? That prompted the most thought? How might asking questions affect understanding of a reading passage? Is this a strategy (formulating questions from a reading) you might use in other classes? For what purposes?

QUESTION, QUESTION

Purpose: Engages students in thinking about a topic, forming true questions, and assessing the quality of questions.

Preparation: Before this structure is introduced to students, the teacher should have established the importance of questions to learning, the idea of different cognitive levels of questions, and the difference between "true" questions and "school" questions, for which an answer is known before it is posed. Before class, the teacher should consider where, during the lesson, he will stop to use this strategy.

Facilitation: At a predetermined point in the lesson, ask students to form pairs. Ask them, with their partners, to identify something they found interesting in the lesson and, together, to create one or two questions for discussion. The first few times you use this strategy, provide question stems that students can use to write a question, such as these:

- I wonder about . . .
- I wonder why . . .
- How are these alike and different?
- How is this like _____?
- What might happen if . . .
- What are the key elements of . . .
- What are the implications of . . .
- What might the consequences be if . . .

Once each pair has formed a question, ask for a volunteer pair to present their question and discuss it with the class.

Deepening thinking about questioning: After several questions have been posed, talk with the class about what constitutes qualities of effective discussion questions—for example, they are open-ended, with more than one correct answer; they are interesting to students; they relate to students' lives; and they help students think about the topic from a different perspective in order to explore the topic more deeply.

ROUND-ROBIN QUESTIONING

Purpose: Gives students practice in writing and posing quality questions and using wait times and verbal prompts with peers, as appropriate.

Preparation: Before using the strategy, help students understand the relationship between learning and asking questions. Hopefully, a norm has been established in the class to encourage student questions; engagement in this activity will provide experience in students' formulating and posing questions.

As part of a reading assignment, ask students to create five questions about the reading: four questions for which they know the answer and one question for which they do not know the answer (i.e., a true question). Initially, this could be done in cooperative groups to provide aid to students who have difficulty accomplishing this task.

Facilitation: Explain the process to students. The teacher will select a student to ask one of her questions. That student will pose the question, wait for three to five seconds, and name a student to respond, waiting again for three to five seconds after the student response to provide feedback. If the answer is correct, the student should acknowledge it. If the answer is somewhat correct, the student should elicit more information by asking questions such as, *Can you tell me why you think that? How did you get your answer?* or *Can you say more about that?* If the answer is incorrect, the student should provide cues to the responding student to help that student come to the correct answer. For example: *If you look on page 36, in the first paragraph, you will see what the character was after.*

When the questioning episode is concluded, the responding student will pose one of his questions, wait three to five seconds, and call on a student to respond, following the same sequence. This should continue until most important facts or understandings have been asked about. Finally, a student should pose one of her true questions and see if a discussion will ensue. The teacher may want to provide sample prompts for students (on cue cards) to use when answers are incorrect.

Debrief With Students

Was this an activity they liked? Why or why not? How might they modify the activity before they use it again?

SAY SOMETHING

Purpose: Helps learners process a reading, increases comprehension by allowing readers time to think through a passage by talking about it, and creates connections by having learners connect a reading passage with prior knowledge.

Preparation: Identify a short reading that is on a topic of interest and that might stimulate discussion and dialogue.

Facilitation: Direct students into pairs and provide each with a copy of the reading passage. Give instructions: *I'll ask you to read a short passage. As soon as you have finished, turn to your partner and "say something" about what that passage means to you. Then listen as your partner says something to you about the same passage. There are no right or wrong things to say; you may ask a question, agree, or disagree with the reading.* Assign a part of the reading. After participants have read and talked, call time. Give them another passage. Continue until the reading has been completed.

Tips

1. This activity works very well with a bulleted list of items. Ask students to read two or three of the bulleted items and talk about them; then assign another two or three. Continue until they have read and discussed the entire list.

2. Alternatively, a series of four or five thought-provoking quotes works well. Ask students to read and say something about the first quote. Continue to call time and assign a new quote until they have read and discussed them all.

SYNECTICS

Purpose: Engages students in metaphorical thinking about the topic under study, facilitates creative thinking that stimulates group discussion, and helps students see a topic from more than one perspective.

Preparation: Prepare a prompt around the topic under study. For example, the prompt might be, *Describe your vision of an effective political campaign.* Select four words or images that participants can use to create metaphors (see examples provided). Put each word or image on a separate sheet of flip-chart paper. Post one in each corner of the room, along with a flip-chart marker.

Facilitation: Present the prompt and ask participants to individually write their responses. After adequate time for individual thinking, ask, "As you think about this topic, is it more like _____ or _____ or _____ or _____ (name the four metaphors)?" For example: *Is an effective political campaign more like an amusement park, the Olympics, an MP3 player, or a buffet?* Ask each student to select the one metaphor that best matches his thinking on the topic.

Once students have selected a metaphor, direct them to move to the corner of the room that displays their chosen metaphor. After they have grouped with others who selected the same metaphor, tell them to list the reasons for their choice on the flip-chart paper (that is, to tell how their selected metaphor is like the topic under consideration).

After adequate time to brainstorm and record, ask each of the four groups to share their ideas with the others. Move to a large-group discussion on the topic.

Sample Metaphors

- Earth, wind, fire, water
- Blue, red, green, yellow
- Coaching basketball, directing a movie, working retail, managing a restaurant
- Shopping mall, movie theater, coffee shop, sports arena
- Pickup truck, Cadillac, SUV, sports car
- Country music, rap, hard rock, jazz

Variations: Simple synectics involves choosing two contrasting items and asking participants to respond individually, in writing, and then to share their ideas in small groups. For example, you might ask one of these questions: *Are algebraic equations more like spaghetti or ice cream? Is the structure of a cell more like fall or spring? Is politics more like a roller coaster or an 18-wheel truck?*

TABLE ROUNDS

Purpose: Establishes a setting that encourages students to think about and discuss important ideas, contributing from their own perspectives and building on one another's ideas to create new understandings; scaffolds true dialogue; and creates a "whole" of collective thinking about a given topic as students share insights through a structured process designed to foster understanding and spark creativity.

Preparation: Identify three or four important topics. For each topic, prepare a set of questions that will guide conversations for participants at each table. Make a copy of the question set, and place it on the table. Provide a variety of markers and crayons as well as one or two sheets of easel paper to form a tablecloth on which participants can record their conversation ideas.

Facilitation: Once four to six students are seated at each table, introduce the process. Explain that each table has been given a topic, with a set of questions to guide conversation. Each table should begin by having someone read the set of questions aloud as others in the small group listen and focus on the important issues. As they talk about their topic, group members will record their responses with markers on the tablecloth. Encourage them to be creative and to use words, pictures, colors, and other visuals. Group members should also verbalize their responses. Instruct them to speak openly and honestly, to listen to others carefully to fully understand their points of view, to watch for connections between ideas, and to honor silence (i.e., to use wait time as appropriate).

When time is called, each group will identify one person to remain as table host. The host's role is to welcome new people to the table, answer any questions about the prior conversations held at the table, and remind people to write down their ideas and questions—not merely to talk to one another—and to make connections between ideas.

Other group members will disperse to different tables so that participants will be with different people for each round of conversation. During the second round, most people (with the exception of the table host) will be talking about a new set of questions. Encourage students to listen to the questions, review the ideas on the tablecloth, discuss them, and add their own ideas.

Modification: For very young students, you may introduce this process by giving them a problem that has multiple solutions; then, rather than a discussion, students will be generating possible solutions. For example, we visited a classroom where the second graders were learning about equations. The teacher gave each group a tablecloth with a number in the center (e.g., 23). She asked each group to write on the paper equations that could form the number in the center of their paper. The students enthusiastically wrote different equations, talking with one another about additional possibilities. It was a creative modification of the strategy that worked well with young children.

Modified from the World Café process (see Brown & Isaacs, 2005).

THINKATHON

Purpose: Engages students for a variety of purposes: solving problems, generating ideas, and reacting to others' ideas.

Preparation: Formulate several open-ended questions related to the topic under study. Write each one on a piece of easel paper, and post the papers around the room. Place several flip-chart markers near each station. Divide participants into teams (one team for each question).

Facilitation: Assign a team to each question. Direct students to gather at the posted easel paper that displays their question, brainstorm answers, and record ideas on the easel paper. After sufficient time, all teams will move to the next station, rotating clockwise. As teams approach a question that has previously been answered by another team, their job is to read through the answers, placing checkmarks next to those with which they agree and adding additional comments or responses. When the teams have rotated through all the stations, they return to their original question, read what others have added, and summarize the class's thinking about their assigned question.

Variation: After the team responds to the first question, they select a team member to stay behind and explain their thinking to visiting teams. This team member's job is to record comments and additional ideas.

THINK-PAIR-SHARE

Purpose: To engage all students in a class with answering a question; to provide time for students to clarify their own thoughts before participating in a large-group discussion; and to help students process information by talking and listening to a partner, making personal meaning, and connecting the new information to prior knowledge.

Preparation: Decide on strategic times to use this process to engage students in thinking about a topic. The strategy can be used effectively before, during, or after a presentation; it is especially good to use prior to a large-group discussion. Decide how you will pair participants and create the prompt that will begin the discussion.

Facilitation: As implied by the title, this activity is carried out in three parts. Pose a question and ask all participants to *think* about it—usually through writing to a prompt or a question. Then ask them to *pair* with another participant to talk about their ideas. Finally, when everyone has had time to think individually and talk about her ideas with a partner, the pairs *share* with the larger group.

TUNING PROTOCOL

Purpose: Encourages intentional and deliberate reflection about a specific work process or product through a protocol of talking and listening, in turn, with peers. The process of thinking aloud moves the reflection to a deeper and more meaningful level. Adherence to the steps of a protocol provides a low-risk environment and limits defensiveness.

Preparation: This protocol can be used for many purposes. Here we share how it has been used by students to assess their own and others' writing. Give students a specific target for a writing assignment: paragraph transitions, a powerful opening sentence, descriptive phrases, metaphors, and so forth. Group students into pairs and then into groups of four.

Facilitation: Review (or introduce) the steps of the process. Lead the class through the following six steps, announcing the amount of time to be allowed for each:

1. **Reflection:** Within each grouping of four students, two students read their writing samples to one another and comment to one another on what they hoped to accomplish related to the target and how well they believe they did, along with evidence for that assessment. The other pair in the group listens but does not talk. Allow an adequate amount of time for each student to read and comment.

2. **Warm Feedback:** The pair that was listening talks to each other—not directly to the readers. They provide positive (or warm) feedback about what they heard that was related to the target. During this time, the readers *listen but do not talk.*

3. **Cool Feedback:** As soon as the pair is finished with the warm feedback, they move to cool feedback, or suggestions for improvement. Again, they talk to each other, not directly to the readers, who are listening in on the conversation. This should be modeled by the teacher prior to students participating. Cool feedback is most effectively posed as questions rather than statements—for example, *I wonder if it would have been stronger to have used a dark image in the opening sentence?*

4. **Reflection:** The initial readers reflect on what they heard and what they learned, both through their own reflection and from listeners' comments. Others *listen but do not talk.*

5. **Switch Roles:** Now the listening pair reads their writing samples to one another and comments, hearing both warm and cool feedback, and reflecting on what they have learned.

6. **Debrief:** Finish the protocol with a discussion of how it went— what went well and what didn't, how students might want to change the next protocol session, and what was learned.

Tip: This process increases in value with repetition. As groups become used to the process, there will be less need for the teacher to facilitate the proess; however, initially, a facilitator can help a group follow the suggested protocol.

Adapted from Looking at Student Work protocols; for additional information about this and other protocols for looking at student work, visit lasw.org.

Resource B

Sample Tools for Formative Assessment

MAKING PERSONAL MEANING

As a unit is being introduced, ask students to respond to four prompts:

1. In my own words, I think this learning goal is about the following:

2. I already know the following things related to this learning goal:

3. I think the following vocabulary words are related to this topic:

4. I have had the following experiences (in school or out of school) that have helped me learn about this goal:

ONE-WORD SUMMARY

1. Summarize content in one word (from reading, presentation, project, or class discussion).

2. Write a paragraph explaining why that word was selected.

Student responses to these prompts can be used effectively as an exit pass from class. Teachers can learn the following kinds of things: (1) where students are in their thinking, (2) common misconceptions or mistaken ideas, (3) trends or patterns in the most frequent ideas from students, (4) unique words and rationales. Teachers then have the opportunity to give feedback to the entire class in summary form—for example, by reporting the most frequent word mentioned, the most unusual word, and the most convincing rationale. They can also give feedback to those students who did not seem to grasp major concepts by pulling aside a group for additional instruction. *I noticed that you turned in a summary at the end of class; however, I'd like to hear you talk more about the major ideas that were included in that lesson. Do you remember yesterday's presentation and discussion? Do you have notes that would help you remember?* As students talk in a small group, they may collectively remember some key points. But it may become clear that they need additional instruction. Alternatively, they may need a new learning strategy to help them understand and internalize information from such a lesson. Teachers might ask, *What strategies did you use during the presentation yesterday?* and *What might you try during the next presentation?*

One-Word Summary also provides teachers with feedback about instructional effectiveness. As a teacher, you may realize that students would benefit from additional opportunities to reflect and verbalize. You may use some different strategies, such as stopping more frequently for Think-Pair-Share during a presentation and asking students to summarize a shorter piece of material in a phrase and/or a word to build successful experience in this type of summarizing activity.

This kind of task is not merely an assessment; it is also an integral part of instruction. In order to complete the One-Word Summary, students must think in order to answer. This reflection to select a word that summarizes the content into a single word will strengthen understanding; writing a paragraph to defend their thinking will help them explore their thinking even further. Writing, like speaking, is a way to think.

CONTINUOUS SELF-MONITORING OF UNDERSTANDING

Give each student three index cards or plastic cups—one each of green, yellow, and red. Help students learn how to monitor their own understanding of the topic under study or discussion. If they are with you, they should display green for "go." If they are somewhat unsure, yellow sends that signal. A red message means "I'm lost." Teachers can scan the class and get a sense of where students think they are at any given time during a lesson.

SELF-ASSESSMENT: HOW WELL DO I UNDERSTAND?

At the end of a presentation or class period, ask students to rate themselves on how well they understand the material, ranging from 5 (understand completely) to 1 (have very little understanding), and then to write a couple of sentences to justify their rating. This form of self-assessment should work in any content area.

1. How well do you understand how to change a meal (and recipes) to serve 4 people into one that serves 12?

2. How well do you understand the literary genres we discussed today?

3. How well do you understand how to multiply and divide fractions?

4. How well do you understand velocity?

5. How well do you understand analogies?

SUMMARY AND QUESTIONS

The following two prompts will not take long for students to answer—either in writing on scrap paper at the end of the period or by e-mail or wiki from home. Ask, *What was the most important thing that you learned today in our class?* and *What questions do you have about the topic under study?*

Other variations of this include a handout with three geometric shapes and the following questions:

1. What are three ideas that you remember from today's class? (triangle)

2. What two ideas square with what you already knew? (square)

3. What one question is circling around in your mind? (circle)

Or you might write three questions on the graphic of a traffic light:

1. What ideas did you already know? (green light)

2. What idea confuses you—and makes you want to stop? (red light)

3. What idea makes you want to slow down in order to learn more? (yellow light)

ASSESSING SKILL IN PROBLEM SOLVING

Instead of giving an entire page of problems for homework in an algebra class, for example, select three that will be challenging but doable by most students. Ask students to solve all three problems and then select one problem for which they write a full explanation of the problem-solving process used. Pose the assignment as follows: *Write out a step-by-step solution to the problem you choose. Divide your paper in half. On the left side, write the first step mathematically. On the right side, in complete sentences, write the process in words. Use words that would be understandable to a pre-algebra student. Be ready to talk about the process tomorrow in class.*

THINKING ROUTINES

Available at Harvard's Project Zero Visible Thinking website (http://www.pz.harvard.edu/vt/VisibleThinking_html_files/03_Thinking Routines/03a_ThinkingRoutines.html)

More than 20 thinking routines are presented on this website. All are simple to use, easy to teach, and encouraging of thinking. Here are two examples:

I Used to Think . . . Now I Think

This thinking routine helps students formulate how their thoughts about a subject have changed as a result of reading, discussing, writing, and so forth. It can be used in a variety of settings—as encouragement of student self-assessment, reflection, and metacognition.

Think, Puzzle, Explore

Much like KWL, this thinking routine helps students think about what they currently believe, what is confusing, and how they think they might explore a topic further by answering three questions: (1) What do you think you know about this topic? (2) What questions or puzzles do you have? and (3) How can you explore this topic?

CHAIN NOTES

Write a topic or a question at the top of a piece of paper and circulate it through the classroom. As a student receives it, she should read through the comments that have been written and add her own thinking or comment about the subject. Students can introduce new ideas or build on existing ones. The question might best relate to an essential question after the class has studied it (e.g., *How does society change?* or *What are the characteristics of living plants?*).

FACT FIRST QUESTIONING

In any subject area, teachers want to see if students know more than the facts; they want to determine if students *understand* the knowledge. This strategy is very simple. Take a fact question and make a statement. Then pose a question about the fact—one that challenges students to go deeper and express more about the content in question.

> Instead of asking, *When did the Civil War end?* (to get the answer 1865), say this: *The Civil War ended in 1865. What other important events took place during that year? Why were they important?*

> Instead of asking, *What kind of rock is sandstone?* (to get the answer sedimentary rock), ask this: *Why is sandstone considered a sedimentary rock?*

> Instead of asking, *What is the area of a rectangle that is 8 feet by 5 feet?* (to get the answer 40 square feet), ask this: *Imagine you had 26 feet of fencing. What is the largest area you could create with that fencing if you wanted to create a pen for your dog?*

RECIPROCAL PEER QUESTIONING

Students question one another about the content they have been studying. Typically, the questions are open-ended, higher-level questions. The teacher might initially give a prompt to which students individually respond in writing—for example, *Think about what you have learned about _____ over the past few days. Write down two or three questions that you would like to ask in order to extend your thinking.* After a couple of minutes of quiet writing and reflection, students gather in pairs or triads and take turns posing their questions. The teacher monitors and selects questions to share with the large group.

References

Ainsworth, L. A., & Viegut, D. (2006). *Common formative assessments: How to connect standards-based instruction and assessment.* Thousand Oaks, CA: Corwin.

Anderson, L. W., & Krathwohl, D. R. (Eds.). (2001). *A taxonomy for learning, teaching, and assessing: A revision of Bloom's taxonomy of educational objectives.* New York, NY: Addison Wesley Longman.

Baker, L. (2005). Developmental differences in megacognition: Implications for metacognitively oriented reading instruction. In S. E. Israel, C. C. Block, K. L. Bauserman, & K. Kinnucan-Welsch (Eds.), *Metacognition in literacy learning: Theory, assessment, instruction, and professional development* (pp. 61–81). Mahwah, NJ: Lawrence Erlbaum.

Bandura, A. (2005). Exercise of personal and collective efficacy in changing societies. In A. Bandura (Ed.), *Self-efficacy in changing societies* (pp. 1–45). Cambridge, UK: Cambridge University Press.

Barell, J. (1995). *Teaching for thoughtfulness: Classroom strategies to enhance intellectual development* (2nd ed.). White Plains, NY: Longman.

Barell, J. (2003). *Developing more curious minds.* Alexandria, VA: Association of Supervision and Curriculum Development.

Barnette, J. J., Walsh, J. A., Orletsky, S. R., & Sattes, B. D. (1995). Staff development for improved classroom questioning and learning. *Research in the Schools, 2*(1), 1–10.

Black, P., Harrison, C., Lee, C., Marshall, B., & Wiliam, D. W. (2003). *Assessment for learning: Putting it into practice.* Maidenhead, UK: Open University Press.

Black, P., & Wiliam, D. (1998a). Assessment and classroom learning. *Assessment in Education, 5*(1), 7–74.

Black, P., & Wiliam, D. (1998b). Inside the black box: Raising standards through classroom assessment. *Phi Delta Kappan, 80*(2), 139–149.

Bloom, B. S. (1956). *Taxonomy of educational objectives: Book 1. Cognitive domain.* New York, NY: Longman.

Bransford, J. E., Brown, A. L., & Cocking, R. R. (Eds.). (2000). *How people learn: Brain, mind, experience, and school.* Washington, DC: National Academy Press.

Brown, J., & Isaacs, D. (2005). *The world café: Shaping our futures through conversations that matter.* San Francisco, CA: Berrett-Koehler.

Chen, M. (2010). *Education nation: Six leading edges of innovation in our schools.* San Francisco, CA: Jossey-Bass.

Christenbury, L., & Kelly, P. (1983). *Questioning: A path to critical thinking.* Urbana, IL: ERIC Clearinghouse on Reading and Communication Skills and the National Council of Teachers of English.

City, E. A., Elmore, R. F., Fiarman, S. E., & Teitel, L. (2009). *Instructional rounds in education.* Cambridge, MA: Harvard Educational Press.

Cohen, D., Raudenbush, S., & Ball, D. (2003). Resources, instruction, and research. *Educational Evaluation and Policy Analysis, 25,* 119–142.

Conley, D. T. (2005). *College knowledge: What it really takes for students to succeed and what we can do to get them ready.* San Francisco, CA: Jossey-Bass.

Costa, A. L., & Kallick, B. (Eds.). (2000). *Activating and engaging habits of mind.* Alexandria, VA: Association for Supervision and Curriculum Development.

Darling-Hammond, L., Barron, B., Pearson, P. D., Schoenfeld, A. H., Stage, E. K., Zimmerman, T. D., . . . Tilson, J. L. (2008). *Powerful learning: What we know about teaching for understanding.* San Francisco, CA: Jossey-Bass.

Deal, T. E., & Peterson, K. D. (2009). *Shaping school culture: Pitfalls, paradoxes, and promises* (2nd ed.). San Francisco, CA: Jossey-Bass.

Dillon, J. T. (1983). *Teaching and the art of questioning.* Bloomington, IN: Phi Delta Kappa.

Dillon, J. T. (1988). *Questioning and teaching: A manual of practice.* New York, NY: Teachers College Press.

Dweck, C. S. (2006). *Mindset: The new psychology of success.* New York, NY: Random House.

Erickson, H. L. (2002). *Concept-based curriculum and instruction.* Thousand Oaks, CA: Corwin.

Fisher, D., & Frey, N. (2007). *Checking for understanding: Formative assessment techniques for your classroom.* Alexandria, VA: Association for Supervision and Curriculum Development.

Fried, R. L. (1995). *The passionate teacher.* Boston, MA: Beacon Press.

Fried, R. L. (2005). *The game of school: Why we all play it, how it hurts kids, and what it will take to change it.* San Francisco, CA: Jossey-Bass.

Gall, M. D. (1984). Synthesis of research on teachers' questioning. *Educational Leadership, 42*(3), 40–47.

Gardner, H. (2006). *Five minds for the future.* Boston, MA: Harvard Business School Press.

Gavelek, J. R., & Raphael, T. E. (1985). Metacognition, instruction, and the role of questioning activities. In D. L. Forest-Pressley, G. E. Mackinnon, & T. G. Waller (Eds.), *Metacogntion, cognition and human performance* (pp. 103–136). Orlando, FL: Academic Press.

Greenstein, L. (2010). *What teachers really need to know about formative assessment.* Alexandria, VA: Association of Supervision and Curriculum Development.

Guskey, T. R. (2007). Using assessments to improve teaching and learning. In D. Reeves (Ed.), *Ahead of the curve: The power of assessment to transform teaching and learning.* Bloomington, IN: Solution Tree.

Harmin, M. (1994). *Inspiring active learning: A handbook for teachers.* Alexandria, VA: Association for Supervision and Curriculum Development.

Hattie, J. (2009). *Visible learning: A synthesis of over 800 meta-analyses relating to achievement.* London: Routledge.

Heritage, H. M. (2010). *Formative assessment: Making it happen in the classroom.* Thousand Oaks, CA: Corwin.

Hess, D. E. (2009). *Controversy in the classroom: The democratic power of discussion.* New York, NY: Routledge.

Holyoak, K. J., & Morrison, R. G. (Eds.). (2005). *The Cambridge handbook of thinking and reasoning.* Cambridge, UK: Cambridge University Press.

Hopkins, K. R. (2010). *Teaching how to learn in a what-to-learn culture.* San Francisco, CA: Jossey-Bass.

Huebner, T. A. (2009). Encouraging girls to pursue math and science. *Educational Leadership, 67*(1), 90–91.

Hunkins, F. P. (1995). *Teaching thinking through effective questioning* (2nd ed.). Norwood, MA: Christopher-Gordon.

Israel, S. E., & Massey, D. (2005). Metacognitive think-alouds: Using a gradual release model with middle school students. In S. E. Israel, C. Collines, K. L. Bauserman, & K. Kinnucan-Welsch (Eds.), *Metacognition in literacy learning: Theory, assessment, instruction, and professional development* (pp. 183–198). Mahwah, NJ: Lawrence Erlbaum.

Johnson, D. W., & Johnson, R. T. (1999). *Learning together and alone: Cooperative, competitive, and individualistic learning* (5th ed.). Boston, MA: Allyn & Bacon.

Jones, M. G. (1990). Action zone theory, target students and science classroom interactions. *Journal of Research in Science Teaching, 27*(8), 651–660.

Kobrin, D. (2004). *In there with the kids* (2nd ed.). Alexandria, VA: Association for Supervision and Curriculum Development.

Krajcik, J., & Blumenfeld, P. (2006). Project-based learning. In R. K. Sawyer (Ed.), *Cambridge handbook of the learning sciences* (pp. 317–334). Cambridge, UK: Cambridge University Press.

Leahy, S., Lyon, C., Thompson, M., & Wiliam, D. (2005). Classroom assessment: Minute by minute, day by day. *Educational Leadership, 63*(3), 19–24.

Lemke, C., & Coughlin, E. (2008). The change agents: Technology is empowering 21st century students in four key ways. *Educational Leadership, 67*(1), 54–59.

Linn, M. C. (2009). The knowledge integration perspective on learning and instruction. In R. K. Sawyer (Ed.), *The Cambridge handbook of the learning sciences* (pp. 243–264). Cambridge, UK: Cambridge University Press.

Marzano, R. J. (2007). Designing a comprehensive approach to classroom assessment. In D. Reeves (Ed.), *Ahead of the curve: The power of assessment to transform teaching and learning.* Bloomington, IN: Solution Tree.

Marzano, R. J., & Kendall, J. S. (2006). *The new taxonomy of educational objectives* (2nd ed.). Thousand Oaks, CA: Corwin.

Marzano, R. J., Pickering, D. J., & Pollock, J. E. (2001). *Classroom instruction that works: Research-based strategies for increasing student achievement.* Alexandria, VA: Association for Supervision and Curriculum Development.

Moss, C. M., & Brookhart, S. M. (2009). *Advancing formative assessment in every classroom: A guide for instructional leaders.* Alexandria, VA: Association for Supervision and Curriculum Development.

Nasir, N. S., Roseberry, A. S., Warren, B., & Lee, C. D. (2006). Learning as a cultural process: Achieving equity through diversity. In R. K. Sawyer (Ed.), *The Cambridge handbook of the learning sciences* (pp. 489–504). New York, NY: Cambridge University Press.

National Research Council. (2001). *How people learn: Brain, mind, and experience and school.* Washington, DC: National Academy Press.

Ornstein, A. C. (1988, February). Questioning: The essence of good teaching—Part II. *NASSP Bulletin, 72*(505), 72–80.

Palincsar, A. S., & Brown, A. L. (1984). Reciprocal teaching of comprehension-fostering and monitoring activities. *Cognition and Instruction, 1*, 117–175.

Pellegrino, J.W., Chudowsky, N., & Glaser, R. (2001). *Knowing what students know: The science and design of educational assessment.* Washington, DC: National Academy Press.

Perkins, D. (1992). *Smart schools: Better thinking and learning for every child.* New York, NY: The Free Press.

Perkins, D. (2003, December). Making thinking visible. *New Horizons for Learning*. Retrieved from http://www.newhorizons.org/strategies/thinking/perkins.htm

Pink, D. H. (2009). *Drive: The surprising truth about what motivates us*. New York, NY: Riverhead Books.

Piper, W. (1930). *The little engine that could*. New York, NY: Platt & Munk.

Pitler, H., Hubbell, E. R., Kuhn, M., & Malenoski, K. (2007). *Using technology with classroom instruction that works*. Alexandria, VA: Association for Supervision and Curriculum Development.

Quintana, C., Shin, N., Norris, C., & Soloway, E. (2009). Learning-centered design: Reflections on the past and directions for the future. In R. K. Sawyer (Ed.), *The Cambridge handbook of the learning sciences* (pp. 119–134). Cambridge, UK: Cambridge University Press.

Ritchhart, R., & Perkins, D. N. (2005). Learning to think: The challenges of teaching thinking. In K. J. Holyoak & R. G. Morrison (Eds.), *The Cambridge book of thinking and reasoning* (pp. 775–796). Cambridge, UK: Cambridge University Press.

Rose, C. M., Minton, L., & Arline, C. (2007). *Uncovering student thinking in mathematics: 25 formative assessment probes*. Thousand Oaks, CA: Corwin.

Rosenshine, B., Meister, C., & Chapman, S. (1996). Teaching students to generate questions: A review of the intervention studies. *Review of Educational Research, 66*(2), 181–221.

Rotherham, A. J., & Willingham, D. (2009). 21st century skills: The challenges ahead. *Educational Leadership, 67*(1), 16–21.

Rowe, M. B. (1986). Wait time: Slowing down may be a way of speeding up! *Journal of Teacher Education, 37*(1), 43–50.

Sadker, D., & Sadker, M. (1985). Is the OK classroom OK? *Phi Delta Kappan, 66*(5), 358–361.

Sawyer, R. K. (2009). The new science of learning. In R. K. Sawyer (Ed.), *The Cambridge handbook of the learning sciences* (pp. 1–16). Cambridge, UK: Cambridge University Press.

Schlechty, P. C. (2002). *Working on the work: An action plan for teachers, principals, and superintendents*. San Francisco, CA: Jossey-Bass.

Schmoker, M. (2011). *Focus: Elevating the essentials to radically improve student learning*. Alexandria, VA: Association for Supervision and Curriculum Development.

Schunk, D. H., & Zimmerman, B. J. (Eds.). (1998). *Self-regulated learning*. New York, NY: Guilford Press.

Secretary's Commission on Achieving Necessary Skills. (1991, June). *What work requires of schools: A SCANS report for America 2000*. Washington, DC: Author.

Sergiovanni, T. (2005). *The lifeworld of leadership: Creating culture, community, and personal meaning in schools*. San Francisco, CA: Jossey-Bass.

Silbey, R. (2002, April). Math think-alouds: Build essential daily math skills through verbal problem solving. *Scholastic Instructor*. Retrieved from http://www2.scholastic.com/browse/article.jsp?id=3584

Sprenger, M. (2005). *How to teach students to remember*. Alexandria, VA: Association for Supervision and Curriculum Development.

Sprenger, M. (2009). Focusing the digital brain. *Educational Leadership, 67*(1), 34–39.

Stiggins, R. J., Arter, J. A., Chappuis, J., & Chappuis, S. (2006). *Classroom assessment for student learning*. Portland, OR: Educational Testing Service.

Swartz, R. J., Costa, A. L., Beyer, B. K., Reagan, R., & Kallick, B. (2008). *Thinking-based learning: Activating students' potential.* Norwood, MA: Christopher-Gordon.

Swicegood, P. R., & Parsons, J. L. (1989). Better questions and answers equal success. *Teaching Exceptional Children, 21*(3), 4–8.

Tishman, S., Perkins, D., & Jay, E. (1995). *The thinking classroom: Learning and teaching in a culture of thinking.* Boston, MA: Allyn & Bacon.

Tobin, K. (1987). The role of wait time in higher cognitive level learning. *Review of Educational Research, 57,* 69–95.

Video Journal in Education. (1999). *Questioning to stimulate learning and thinking: Elementary and secondary versions.* Sandy, UT: School Improvement Network.

Vygotsky, L. (1978). *Mind in society: The development of higher psychological processes.* Cambridge, MA: Harvard University Press.

Wagner, T. (2008). *The global achievement gap: Why even our best schools don't teach the new survival skills our children need—and what we can do about it.* New York, NY: Basic Books.

Walsh, J. A., & Sattes, B. D. (2005). *Quality questioning: Research-based practice to engage every learner.* Thousand Oaks, CA: Corwin.

Wassermann, S. (2009). *Teaching for thinking today: Theory, strategies, and activities for the K–8 classroom.* New York, NY: Teachers College Press.

Webb, N. L. (2002, March 28). *Depth-of-knowledge levels for four content areas.* Retrieved from http://facstaff.wcer.wisc.edu/normw/All%20content%20areas%20%20DOK%20levels%2032802.doc

Wells, G. (2001). The case for dialogic inquiry. In G. Wells (Ed.), *Action, talk and text: Learning and teaching through inquiry* (pp. 171–185). New York, NY: Teachers College Press.

White, E. B. (1952). *Charlotte's web.* New York, NY: Harper-Collins.

Willingham, D. T. (2009). *Why don't students like school? A cognitive scientist answers questions about how the mind works and what it means for the classroom.* San Francisco, CA: Jossey-Bass.

Zimmerman, B. J. (1998). Developing self-fulfilling cycles of academic regulation: An analysis of exemplary instructional models. In D. Schunk & B. J. Zimmerman (Eds.), *Self-regulated learning: From teaching to self-reflective practice* (pp. 1–19). New York, NY: Guilford Press.

Index

Note: In page references, f indicates figures and i indicates illustrations.

CORWIN

A SAGE Company

The Corwin logo—a raven striding across an open book—represents the union of courage and learning. Corwin is committed to improving education for all learners by publishing books and other professional development resources for those serving the field of PreK–12 education. By providing practical, hands-on materials, Corwin continues to carry out the promise of its motto: **"Helping Educators Do Their Work Better."**